PENTECOST 2

proclamation

Interpreting
the Lessons
of the
Church Year

James L. Boyce

PENTECOST 2

PROCLAMATION 6 | SERIES C

FORTRESS PRESS | MINNEAPOLIS

PROCLAMATION 6
Interpreting the Lessons of the Church Year
Series C, Pentecost 2

Cover design: Ellen Maly
Text design: David Lott

The Library of Congress has cataloged the first four volumes of Series A as follows:

Proclamation 6, Series A: interpreting the lessons of the church
    year.
        p.   cm.
    Contents: [1] Advent/Christmas / J. Christiaan Beker — [2]
Epiphany / Susan K. Hedahl — [3] Lent / Peter J. Gomes — [4] Holy
Week / Robin Scroggs.
    ISBN 0-8006-4207-4 (v. 1 : alk. paper) — ISBN 0-8006-4208-2 (v.
2 : alk. paper) — ISBN 0-8006-4209-0 (v. 3 : alk. paper) — ISBN 0-8006-4210-4
(v. 4 : alk. paper).
    1. Bible—Homiletical use. 2. Bible—liturgical lessons,
English.
BS534.5P74   1995
251—dc20   95-4622
                                                                CIP
        Series C:
        Advent/Christmas / E. Elizabeth Johnson—ISBN 0-8006-4231-7
        Epiphany / Richard I. Pervo—ISBN 0-8006-4232-5
        Lent / Bernhard W. Anderson —ISBN 0-8006-4233-3
        Holy Week / Patricia Wilson-Kastner—ISBN 0-8006-4234-1
        Easter / L. William Countryman—ISBN 0-8006-4235-X
        Pentecost 1 / Terence E. Fretheim—ISBN 0-8006-4236-8
        Pentecost 2 / James L. Boyce—ISBN 0-8006-4237-6
        Pentecost 3 / William L. Holladay—ISBN 0-8006-4238-4

Manufactured in the U. S. A.   AF 1-4237

01   00   99   98   97   1   2   3   4   5   6   7   8   9   1

Contents

Introduction
The Journey of Discipleship

Recent biblical studies have newly impressed upon the interpreter and preacher how important it is to be guided by a perspective of the whole. Thus, when the texts assigned for the Sundays of the church year invite focus on smaller units, it is extremely helpful, even necessary, for the preacher's perspective to be shaped and guided by the framework and movement of the larger context.

This is especially true for the Gospel lessons assigned for the second portion of the season of Pentecost in the year of Luke. It has become almost a commonplace to identify the portion of Luke from which all the lessons for these Sundays come as Luke's "travel narrative," the "journey to Jerusalem," or "the way of the determined Messiah" (D. Tiede, *Luke*, ACNT [Minneapolis: Augsburg, 1988], 30 [9:51—19:27]). Familiarity does not make this awareness trivial. In 9:51 we read, "When the days drew near for him to be taken up, he set his face to go to Jerusalem." These words set the theme and design for Jesus' "journey" to Jerusalem—the eventual arrest, trial, crucifixion, and the surprising announcement of the resurrection and ascension shape the narrative throughout. A further theme is suggested in the issue of receiving or not receiving this Jesus (9:53) precisely because of his purposive direction toward Jerusalem. The obviously linked issue of discipleship is pressed in the back-to-back episodes about "following" Jesus that occur in 9:57-61 and culminate in the saying about the forward-looking and purposive nature of discipleship and the kingdom of God: "No one who puts a hand to the plow and looks back is fit for the kingdom of God" (9:62). Along the way constant reminders of the "journey" accompany the narratives of Jesus' healings, parables, and other teachings. They are meant to invite us modern readers and hearers along with the Twelve not only to reflect on but to experience what it means to accompany Jesus on the faithful and often surprising "journey of discipleship."

Two narratives—unfortunately completely missing from the lectionary for the year of Luke—are important as thematic paradigms for Luke's overall perspective and so for this journey: the juxtaposed stories of the healing of the paralytic and the call of Levi the tax collector (5:17-26; 27-32). In the first, healing is bound together with the issue of the forgiveness of sins and of Jesus' authority *on earth* to forgive sins. When in the immediately following story, Levi, a "tax collector and sinner," is called to "follow me," we know that we are in for some surprises. Both of these stories are at the heart of Luke's story. In the power of the Spirit at work in Jesus' ministry, in the linking of forgiveness and healing, is the sign and declaration for the Lukan disciple community of the impossibility of new wine being contained in old wine skins (5:37).

At the birth of Jesus (2:11), and again at the end of this "journey" with the encounter with Zacchaeus in Jericho (19:10) we hear that "today" salvation has happened in this Jesus. Throughout the reading of Luke, and so in the Pentecost "journey of discipleship" the preacher will want to be attentive to the signs of this newness, to the ways in which healing and forgiveness and salvation are constantly bound up together and break in upon our world "this day" with the signs of God's newness.

Tenth Sunday after Pentecost
Seventeenth Sunday in Ordinary Time/Proper 12

Lectionary	First Lesson	Psalm	Second Lesson	Gospel
Revised Common	Gen. 18:20-32 or Hosea 1:2-10	Psalm 138 or 85	Col. 2:6-15, (16-19)	Luke 11:1-13
Episcopal (BCP)	Gen. 18:20-33	Psalm 138	Col. 2:6-15	Luke 11:1-13
Roman Catholic	Gen. 18:20-32	Ps. 138:1-3, 6-8	Col. 2:12-14	Luke 11:1-13
Lutheran (LBW)	Gen. 18:20-32	Psalm 138	Col. 2:6-15	Luke 11:1-13

FIRST LESSON: GENESIS 18:20-32; HOSEA 1:2-10

Genesis 18:20-32. This lesson belongs to the Abraham cycle (Genesis 12–25) in which God's repeated call and promise (for instance, 12:1-3; 15:1-6; 17:1-8) are tested ("sister" Sarai in Egypt, chap. 12; Ishmael, chap. 16). It continues last Sunday's story (18:1-10a) of the three strangers who promise that "Sarah shall have a son" in "advanced age." Today's lesson attends to the second part of their twofold agenda: carrying out the Lord's destruction of Sodom and Gomorrah.

Balanced transitions (cf. "went," 16, 22, 33) divide the narrative (16-33) into two sections linked by key words to the same central theme—God's promise to Abraham (18). In the first section (17-21) the Lord deliberates over the fate of Sodom. Are things really as bad as the reports (20-21)? The conditional language seems to leave the matter open—"if not, I will know" (21)—but the remark about hiding "what I am about to do" leaves little uncertainty. Furthermore, concealment from Abraham would be inconsistent with God's purposes (18-19).

When the second section begins (22-33), it is clear that Abraham knows. The men go "toward Sodom" to complete the Lord's mission, but Abraham "remains standing before the Lord." Confident in covenant intimacy he draws "near" and dares to speak. How just is a God who contemplates the destruction of the righteous along with the wicked? "Far be that from you!" (25). If Abraham is to believe that he is chosen and blessed for doing righteousness and justice (19; cf. 15:6), then he has a stake in the fate of the righteous.

Issues of justice and righteousness and the promises of God thus link the two sections and merge in Abraham's carefully structured intercessions, each beginning with Abraham's "Suppose . . ." and concluding with the Lord's "If I find, I will forgive [not destroy, not do it]." The simple narrative conclusion confirms Abraham's success: the Lord "finished speaking to Abraham; and Abraham returned to his place" (33). Yet not even ten are found so as to avert the destruction. It is tragic when later we hear that Abraham "went early in the morning to the place where he had stood before the Lord" (19:27), though even in the destruction "God remembered Abraham" in the rescue of Lot (19:29).

Though persistence in prayer is suggested by Abraham's sixfold (3 x 2!) petition and its association with today's Gospel, the more clear focus of this lesson is righteousness and justice and the surety of God's promises. Abraham counts on the promise of God and unashamedly takes God at God's word that he will be a blessing for all nations. Abraham's example underscores the invitation of covenant intimacy to wrestle with questions of how God's promises shall be fulfilled in this world. God, too, wrestles here with what that faithfulness means. God enters the fray and negotiates in the give and take of real-life possibilities. God entertains a condition: If . . . then I will. The only surety is God's commitment to the promise.

Hosea 1:2-10. The alternative reading from Hosea is a narrative summary of Hosea's message of judgment and hope, presented in the striking and even jarring metaphor that likens the people of Israel to a woman who has gone "whoring" and borne children out of wedlock. Thus Hosea's message, too, focuses on God's covenant promises and the call for the faithfulness of God's covenant people.

After noting in verbal correspondence Hosea's obedience to God's call ("Go, take. . . . So he went and took," 2-3), vv. 4-9 narrate how Gomer, Hosea's "wife of whoredom," bears three "children of whoredom." Their names are symbolic of impending doom and final separation and abandonment: "Jezreel," recalling the battle plain of conquering enemies (4-5); "Not-pitied"(6-7); and "Not my people" (8-9).

In a whirlwind of reversal and restoration, vv. 10 and 11 introduce a message of salvation and hope. The gathered people as numerous as the sands of the sea and the land repossessed recall the promises to Abraham. The reversal is sealed in the new names of the children: "Not my people" is now renamed "children of the living God," and "Jezreel" turns from a place of destruction to a symbolic landmark of a land and a people restored.

SECOND LESSON: COLOSSIANS 2:6-15, (16-19)

The "therefore" of v. 6 signals the central theological argument for which the letter's opening has laid the foundation (see 1:12-23 and notes for the Ninth Sunday after Pentecost). The carefully knit christological argument asserts that true wisdom (words for wisdom are plentiful: *epignosis*: 4 times—1:9, 10; 2:2; 3:10 [see the Eleventh Sunday after Pentecost]; *sofia*: 6 times—1:9,

28; 2:3, 23; 3:16; 4:5; *synesis*: 2 times—1:9, 2:2) consists in understanding the "mystery" of God as a "hidden treasure" (2:3), namely, Christ Jesus himself, in whom dwells bodily (9) the very "fullness" of God (*pleroma*, 2:9; see also 1:19). In his humanity as the crucified one and in his resurrected exaltation to the right hand of God (3:1, see the Eleventh Sunday after Pentecost) wisdom recognizes the real and present experience of the firstborn of all creation (1:15) and the center of all reality (1:19, 20; 3:11).

The false teachings of human wisdom (*philosophia*, 2:8) and empty deception (*kene apate*, 2:8; *pithanologia* [that is, deceitfully persuasive argument], 2:4) assign credence and power to "elemental powers of the universe" (*stoicheia tou kosmou*, 2:8, 20) rather than to Christ. But through Christ's power in baptism the Colossians are newly created in the very image of their creator (*kata eikona*, 3:10) and, having put off the old, now exhibit in their lives those attributes appropriate to God's holy and beloved chosen ones (3:12).

The argument is introduced by Paul's ardent prayer (*agona*, struggle, 2:1) that the Colossians be confidently founded and unified (*symbibazo*, 2:2, imagines the ligaments of the body; cf. 2:19 and Eph. 4:16) in true wisdom and not "argued off the straight and narrow" (*paralogizo,* 2:4) by clever arguments.

The language and images of vv. 6-15—dying and rising through baptism, being knit together, walking, growing—recall Rom. 6:1-10 and Eph. 2:1-10; 4:15-16. Wisdom that comes from being "in Christ" ("in him," "with him," 2:7, 9, 11, 12, 13) contrasts human wisdom (*philosophia*, 2:8). We have "received" and are "taught" Christ and then "continue to live" in him (*peripateo*, walk, 6), while other humans actively and deceitfully "pass on" their "empty deceptions" (8). In the real battle for power over people's lives Christ has become the "head" over "every ruler [*arche*; cf. 1:16, 18] and authority [*exousia*, 1:13, 16]."

The key, then, is to "Watch out! Be on guard!" (NRSV's "See to it" is too weak) against such impostors. The metaphors of this life in Christ shift between that of a building under continuous construction (6-7) and a body united in full maturity with Christ as its "head" (8-10). Full maturity rests on the "power of God" (12) experienced through our being linked to Christ's death and resurrection through baptism (12; cf. Rom. 6: 4-7). Baptism marks the move from death to life ("once dead . . . now alive") that has broken the bondage to powers ("in trespasses") and united us in the life of Christ ("together with him") because God has "acted in grace to forgive us all our trespasses" (14; cf. "by grace you have been saved, Eph. 2:5).

Behind vv. 14 and 15 and crucial to their explication stand the events of Christ's crucifixion. The "indictment" (*cheirographon*, not "record") with its "decrees" of death "that stood against us" Christ wiped out by "lifting it up" (that is, on the cross; *airo*) "from the midst" (*ek mesou*; that is, in public) and nailing it to the cross. At the same time it was Christ himself who was lifted up and nailed to the cross, and in that lifting up and nailing to the cross he has become *our indictment*, bodily assuming in his flesh the indictment that was against us and "erasing it completely." By God's raising him from the dead Christ has stripped bare, opened to public disgrace, and lead in triumph those rulers and principalities who were deluded by false hopes of victory at his death. When Jesus was stripped, naked and helpless, it was indeed the powers of this world that were stripped and laid out in public for ridicule. And in that reversal, the cross becomes, under the sign of opposites, the very sign of triumph.

"Therefore," if the power of such rulers is as illusory as the apparent defeat of the cross, which in reality through baptism is God's way of making us alive in Christ, then Paul's exhortation is not to turn back to things that now lie in the past by denying that this new body is continuously supplied, unified, and growing by God's power (16-19).

GOSPEL: LUKE 11:1-13

(*For the text's context see comments in the Introduction.*) Before today's reading in our journey we have accompanied the commissioning and return of the Seventy (10:20); heard Jesus' pronouncement about the blessedness of the disciples (10:21-24); heard the parable of the Good Samaritan in response to a lawyer's question about what it means to be a neighbor in relation to the goal of eternal life (10:25-37); and wrestled with Mary and Martha over choices on the way of discipleship (10:38-42).

The lesson begins with a simple transition bearing a Lukan signature: "And it came to pass . . . Jesus was praying." The subject of "prayer" (nineteen times in Luke's Gospel) is thus signaled as the organizing principle for this collection of Jesus' teaching material on prayer and discipleship in the kingdom.

When Jesus finished—the disciples are careful not to interrupt this activity, important even for Jesus—one of the disciples asks him to teach them how to pray. Acknowledging the appropriateness of his identification as "teacher," Jesus responds not by giving a lecture on prayer but with an object lesson, a ready-made prayer sufficient for every time and place. "Whenever you pray, pray as follows. . . ." The present tense of the three occurrences of the verb of praying in vv. 1-2 underscores the time-enduring quality. The prayer is at once familiar and surprising—familiar as the defining prayer of Christian worship from the beginning; surprising in its brevity and particulars, since Luke's version has never become familiar in cultic expression. A few comments about this version of the prayer:

Simple and direct is the familiar address of God as Father. Also simple is the central double focus on the hallowing of God's name and the coming of the kingdom, perhaps reflecting the double concern of the law—"You shall love God with all your heart, and your neighbor as yourself"—in which the hallowing of God's name and the coming and fulfillment of God's rule are to be recognized. Perhaps the omission of the petition about God's will is understandable on the assumption that, should God's kingdom come, that would be tantamount to the fruition of God's will and purposes.

The prayer for bread is remarkable at two points: the tense of the verb of giving, and the unusual (redundant?) "each day" (*to kath hemeron*). The present tense emphasizes the request for "continual" giving and the "each day" at least underscores the unanimous uncertainty of Christian tradition about just what kind of bread the *epiousion*, traditionally translated "daily," actually refers. Bread "for the morrow" or "for the next day" or bread "of sustenance" are inviting alternatives that would alleviate the uncomfortable redundancy.

The petition about reciprocal forgiveness is familiar, except again in the present tense of the verb that points, not to past actions of forgiveness, as in Matthew's version, but to a continuous disciple lifestyle of forgiving: "Forgive us our sins as we ourselves continue to [or will continue to] forgive everyone who ever has a debt against us."

Finally, the familiar prayer of every faithful disciple: "Do not lead us into a time of testing" that would become the occasion for falling away from faithful discipleship. Other teaching materials of Jesus on prayer follows, linked not by central point or content, but only by the common theme of teaching on prayer.

First is a brief parable about two "friends," one of whom comes seeking assistance on behalf of a third "friend." The occasion for the request and the problem it presents is its inopportune timing. He comes during the night when the door is shut and all are asleep. But the key to the response here is not the traditionally assumed "persistence" of the entreaty. In spite of this traditional interpretation and the NRSV's title "Perseverance in Prayer," there is no mention of perseverance in the story. The petition is granted not on the basis of perseverance or "friendship" but because of his *anaideia*. This word, normally meaning "shamelessness," nowhere else has the meaning of perseverance, unless it has that meaning in this context. Accordingly, it is better to assume that it is precisely because of his shamelessness, his impudence—that is, because he presumes precisely on his relationship of being a *philos*, a "friend"—that the request is honored. Such an interpretation fits better with the content and character of the preceding Lord's prayer, in its invitation to presume on God's favor and relationship and unashamedly come to God in prayer.

Verses 9-10 append a proverbial saying on asking and receiving, seeking and finding, knocking and opening, that asserts the assured response to prayer. Verses 11-13 address the issue of the character of such answers to prayer with the assurance that, when an answer comes, the disciple can trust in the goodness of God to be reflected in its appropriateness. The conclusion is surprising when it announces that what God gives is not just "good gifts" (cf. Matt. 7:11) but the Holy Spirit. For Luke, the object and fruition of the life of prayer, the ultimate gift, is the Spirit who empowers the life of the disciple community.

The traditional interpretation of this passage in terms of persistence in prayer has occasioned its linking with the narrative of Abraham's intercessions. Certainly that approach is possible. The remarks above have suggested another key approach, however. Jesus' sample prayer authorizes the disciple to address God as Father and to trust the promise that in answer to prayer God's name will be hallowed and God's kingdom will indeed come to fruition. Furthermore, the fact that the friend at midnight unashamedly presumes on his "friend" within, points to the relationship upon which that presumption depends. What kind of a God dwells so close to us as to be addressed as Father and friend? What kind of God risks that we should take the promise seriously, and unashamedly and in confidence believe that, whenever we pray, whenever we ask, we shall receive, not just what we ask, but even more than we could ever imagine—the gift of God's Spirit whose pouring out upon all nations we celebrate especially in this Pentecost season.

Eleventh Sunday after Pentecost
Eighteenth Sunday in Ordinary Time/Proper 13

Lectionary	First Lesson	Psalm	Second Lesson	Gospel
Revised Common	Eccl. 1:2, 12-14; 2:18-23 *or* Hosea 11:1-11	Ps. 49:1-12 *or* 107:1-9, 43	Col. 3:1-11	Luke 12:13-21
Episcopal (BCP)	Eccl. 1:12-14; 2:(1-7, 11),18-23	Psalm 49 *or* 49:1-11	Col. 3:(5-11), 12-17	Luke 12:13-21
Roman Catholic	Eccl. 1:2; 2:21-23	Ps. 95:1-2, 6-9	Col. 3:1-5, 9-11	Luke 12:13-21
Lutheran (LBW)	Eccl. 1:2; 2:18-26	Ps. 49:1-11	Col. 3:1-11	Luke 12:13-21

FIRST LESSON: ECCLESIASTES 1:2, 12-14; 2:(1-7, 11), 18-26; HOSEA 11:1-11

Ecclesiastes 1:2, 12-14; 2:(1-7, 11), 18-26. The opening two chapters of these "reflections of a Royal Philosopher" (NRSV, cf. 1:1, 12; identified as Qoheleth from the Hebrew *qhl*; since the Reformation as "Preacher" [RSV], but in more recent scholarship, as "Teacher" [cf. NIV, NRSV]) form a thematically unified statement of the central question of life. They may be divided into sections as follows:

(1) 1:2-3   Theme: "What do people gain?" "All is Vanity"
(2) 1:4-11   Life is cyclical: "Nothing new under the sun"
(3) 1:12-18   Trial/Evaluation I: "Mind applied to Wisdom"
(4) 2:1-11   Trial/Evaluation II: "A test of Pleasure"
(5) 2:12-17   Trial/Evaluation III: "Consider Wisdom, Madness/Folly"
(6) 2:18-23   Trial/Evaluation IV: "All my Toil"
(7) 2:24-26   Summary and Theme: "Eat and drink . . . All is Vanity"

In section one's reversed answer (2) and question (3) format the philosopher frames the question of ultimate happiness, its answer coming immediately in this work's refrain (five times in v. 2, thirty-eight times throughout): All is vanity, utter vanity! All those things to which we give our energies in the quest for happiness are so much "vapor" or "smoke" (Hebrew: *hebel*).

Section two (1:4-11) grounds the theme: generations come and go, but with each turn of the rising and setting of the sun, the philosopher knows the "wearisome" reminder that "what has been will be" and "there is nothing new *under the sun*" (9). The assertion that those who come after will not even remember those who came before leads the philosopher in sections three through six to test several common human proposals for happiness. First (1:12-18), the "teacher" of wisdom ironically applies wisdom to show that even wisdom "is an unhappy business" (13). However great the wisdom, "what is crooked cannot be made straight" (15) and the whole is just no more than smoke (vanity) and a "chasing after wind" (14, 17). Greater wisdom only means more sorrow (18)!

Trial is then made in turn of Pleasure (2:1-11; no pleasure left untried, 10), of wisdom's opposite, Madness or Folly (2:12-17; their end is the same, 16), and of Work (2:18-23). The final verdict in each instance is the same: all is vanity, a chasing after wind, nothing new *under the sun* (1:14, 17; 2:11, 17, 23).

The final section's (2:24-26) invitation thus to "eat and drink, and find enjoyment" (24) may seem to offer some relief from this seeming overwhelming pessimism, especially in the assertion that such pleasures that life does offer come from the hand of God (25). Yet this, too, is a fleeting gain, for in the end "This also is vanity and a chasing after wind" (26). Life is grim and incomprehensible even to one gifted with wisdom; the only hope is to cleave to one's duty, to fear God and to keep the commandments, for all things stand under God's final judgment (12:13-14).

Hosea 11:1-11. After last Sunday's parabolic summary of Hosea's message of God's steadfast love (see the Tenth Sunday after Pentecost) comes this remarkably striking poetic passage in which God addresses Israel directly. As the NRSV format makes clear, in alternating stanzas Yahweh meditates in point and counterpoint in themes of intimacy or closeness (11:1, 3-4) and distance or judgment (11:2, 5-7), escalating to the sudden break and change of heart revealed in fourfold questions (8a-b). Then comes a return to compassion (8c), followed by firm resolution not to execute wrath (9).

In vv. 1 and 2 intimacy and distance alternate. Israel is a child; not just any child, but "my" son, whose "calling" from Egypt implies destiny that goes unfulfilled. For, underscored by the link-word *calling*, intimacy is balanced by increasing distance ("the more I called, the more they went from me . . . to Baals and . . . idols," 2) confirmed in the linguistic move from the singular "child" (1) to the plural "they" (2).

Verses 3 and 4 expand the theme of intimacy and relationship with picturesque and particular detail; the loving "parent" recollects with tender, embracing thoughts the first steps, the child cuddled in arms, feeding time, and the child snuggled against the parent's cheek. The children are led, not with harsh ropes of confinement, but with tender cords of kindness and the bands of love. Yet, even in the midst of intimacy, there is pathos in the reminder that they "did not know" who healed them (3), by which a return to the theme of distance in stanza three (5-7) is anticipated.

Now judgment and distance recur with a deliberate "return" to the land of Egypt from which the child has been "called" (1). Language of parent and child is abandoned for talk of king and subjects. Wanted or not, this people will get a "new king" instead of a loving parent because they "refused" the call to "return" (5) and are bent on "turning away" (7). Sudden harsh language contrasts—swords, raging, cities, consuming, oracle priests, devouring, scheming—as this people's "calls" are not heard by the one whom they have abandoned. A glimmer of hope, in the claim that they are at least "my" people, is dashed in the third-person conclusion: they call to the "Most High" (not "to me") but "he" does not answer by rescuing them (God is not "I" for the first time; cf. vv. 1-6). The distance is complete; judgment has won the day.

The utter distance does not quite prepare for the sudden reversal, but occasions it. Parental compassion will not ultimately let go of the child; in fourfold questions parental love argues against logic. The heart will not abide the destructive judgment logic suggests. Once more compassion suddenly grows warm and tender. There is return to the parent-child of stanza 2. Yet beyond the determined "I will not" (9) the metaphor breaks down. One can compare God's love to human love only so far. "For I am God, and not a mortal." God's love is holy, just, and finally it is steadfast.

In the final stanza's (10-11) images of fearsome strength alongside those of children restored, intimacy and distance stand in tension. These children come trembling before the parental lion's roar of strength and power, but they come knowing that "I" (note the return to the first person from the third person, 10) will return them to their homes. The question remains whether the previous intimacy can be recovered. There is restoration, there is love, but it continues in a new key.

SECOND LESSON: COLOSSIANS 3:1-11, (12-17)

Just as true wisdom knows the centrality of Christ's death ("if you died with Christ," 2:20), so the resurrection is the culminating victory of Christ's life ("if you were raised with Christ," 3:1). This "conclusion" or culmination to the argument of last Sunday's lesson (see the Tenth Sunday after Pentecost) is signaled in the threefold introductory "therefore"s (Greek: *oun*; 3:1, 5, 12) that mark the unit of today's reading (3:1-17) and divide it into three distinct sections (see NIV; the NRSV has masked or ignored these literary signals):

Section 1:	3:1-4	Resurrected life hid with Christ in God
Section 2:	3:5-11	Stripping off the old life
Section 3:	3:12-17	Putting on the new life; thanksgiving

A sense of the whole unit is important for the preacher, though no series includes the whole, either omitting the reference to God's wrath against old evil ways (3:6-8), the whole of section 1's foundation for the exhortation, or, while including the "putting to death" and "stripping off" of section 2, stopping short of including the new clothing and the climax in love, peace, and thanksgiving that come in the doxological conclusion.

In section 1 the themes of death and resurrection ground the exhortation in which earlier themes of the letter are now picked up and applied to present experience. "You have died" (3:3); "you have been raised" (3:1). The indicative states as boldly as anywhere in the New Testament the present reality of the resurrection. That one's life now is "hidden with Christ in God" (3) means power here and now to "set your minds on" (*phroneo*, cf. Matt. 16:23; Rom. 15:5; and esp. Phil. 2:2f.) things above, that is, to have one's whole existence in body, mind, and spirit, brought into such conformity that false wisdom or spirits can no longer control one's life.

A life so real is not about esoteric mysteries but has implications for here and now. Section 2 (5-11) speaks of "putting to death" those earthly "parts" or "accretions," named in two sets of five (3:5, 8), that mark the old "disobedience" deserving of the wrath of God (6). This is not a new self-help program. The "then" and "now" of "stripping off" the old and "clothing yourselves" with the new (9,10) are an explicit verbal recollection of the image of Christ's crucifixion and death (see the Tenth Sunday after Pentecost) by which this new person is empowered and "constantly being renewed" (the verb is present tense) "into" a knowledge (*epignosis*) that is conformed to the image of the one who created it (the verb *ktizo* recalls explicitly 1:15-16 and the image of Christ as the creator of all things). This new knowledge and creation empower a life in which traditional barriers of race, party or group, nationality, and status or class (11) no longer exist (the language and context parallel Gal. 3:27-28, even to the image of being clothed in Christ). Instead, everything (*ta panta*) is bound up in Christ's life (cf. 1:20).

Section 3 (12-17) argues that the new person, chosen, holy, and loved by God (12)—the counterpart to putting to death and stripping off—is putting on the new clothes of compassion and so forth (again parallel in its fivefold content). Rather than the elemental spirits, to which we have died (20), grace is now the dynamic principle of new life; one lives by grace (*charizomai*, translated "forgive") toward one another "just as" the Lord has "graced" you (13). As in 1 Corinthians 13, the crowning new garment ("above all"), that "binds all together" like sinews the body, is love (14; cf. 3:19; Eph. 4:16).

Having arrived at love as the binding capstone for all those who have been put to death and raised again with Christ, the whole argument from

2:8 now resolves in doxology. Themes of "peace" and "thanksgiving" summarize the marks of true wisdom that have been the concern of this epistle. In the indwelling word of Christ will come that kind of mutual teaching and admonishing that consists not in clever arguments but in psalms and hymns and spiritual songs that are taught in the heart "by grace" (*en chariti*) in thanksgiving to God. In this final section (12-17) five occurrences of "grace" (*charis*, masked by their translation as "forgive," "gratitude," or "thanksgiving") form a kind of subtheme for the message. This "grace" makes it so that "whatever you do," every action of word or deed done in the name of the Lord Jesus will redound as the response of grace-filled thanksgiving (indeed the flip side of grace) to God the Father through Christ (17).

GOSPEL: LUKE 12:13-21

The Gospel brings together two teaching pieces for disciples on the journey. In the first (13-15), in response to "someone's" request about dividing an inheritance, Jesus makes a double pronouncement about watchfulness against greed along with the reason such watchfulness is necessary: Because "life is more than abundance of possessions" (cf. 12:33, "Sell your possessions and give alms"; and 12:35-48, with its charge to be prudent stewards of those "possessions" [44] entrusted for management). The second (16-21) is in the form of a parable with concluding moral—"So it is . . ." (21)—in which the actions of a rich man who "stores up treasure for the self" are contrasted with those who are "rich toward God," who recognize that life does not consist in abundance of things (15), that life is more than food, clothing, and other outward things (23).

The Gospel and first lesson alike ponder issues of possessions, true happiness, and the meaning of life. The request to "divide" the inheritance ("divide" and "arbitrator" are forms of the same Greek word "to divide, decide," 13-14), probes who is the rightful "judge" of life, and assigns the "decisive" role to the perspective of heaven.

In light of Ecclesiastes, the landowner can be described as a "fool" only from the perspective of God, who indeed is the only one who addresses him as such. By worldly standards, and so for the reader up to the point of God's address, he would appear the very model of wisdom. Is not the owner to be commended for not acting frivolously, but taking counsel (*dialogizomai*; cf. Luke 14:25-33, the Sixteenth Sunday after Pentecost) and carefully planning for the property entrusted to him? His reasoning presents problem and solution in exemplary pragmatic fashion: old barns replaced by new, provision not only for crops, but protective storage for other goods as well. In his soliloquy we hear echoes of the wise philosopher's counsel: "there is nothing better for mortals than to eat and drink, and find enjoyment in their toil," for "this also is from the hand of God." (Eccl. 2:24; cf. also 3:13, 5:18). His actions are the sum total of what human wisdom has been able to fathom. We do well not to chastise him too quickly.

Yet this parable raises precisely that issue: What does human wisdom teach, and how does that stack up against a more "lofty" perspective? In fact, this parable meditates on the essence of "life" (*psyche*, commonly translated "soul"), in what does it consist and with what quality will one have it. Five times the word appears here in ever-deepening senses, from simple "self," to self that can "eat, drink, and be merry," to the reminder that "life" will come to an end, to the command not to worry about "life" as to body, because "life" is more than food and clothing. This stress on *psyche* links the parable to the teaching material that precedes and follows (22-34; cf. *zoe*, "life" in 12:15; Jesus' words on "saving and losing 'life,'" 9:24; the twofold command to love God with all your "life," 10:27; and the call of disciples to hate mother, spouse, children, siblings, and even "life," 14:36).

Strikingly, the perspective of heaven appears in the character of God whose question matches that of the philosopher of wisdom: death comes to all, whether "this very night" (20) or another, and then to whom will all this "stuff" for which you have labored belong? But, whereas the earlier "teacher" assigns all to "vanity," for Luke's "teacher" the call is to confident assurance about where "true treasure" is to be had. Being "rich toward God" is a treasure that derives from a God who worries about your life, and whose very pleasure and delight is in giving you the kingdom (see the Twelfth Sunday after Pentecost).

All of the lessons call into question so much of that to which our culture encourages us to dedicate our lives. We are defined by the GNP and by standards of production. A static business is a dying business. The bottom line is the key to success and evaluation. But when old age creeps up, when we stand at the sickbed or at the graveside of a loved one or friend, when we ponder the absurd tragedy, violence, and destruction in our world, when we face the limits of our humanity, we are compelled to ask, What is it all for? Is this all there is? The teacher of wisdom calls into question all that so often counts for happiness; death and the endless cycle of life have a way of leveling the playing field for everyone.

Is there any hope, any justice? In this life? After death? The writer of Ecclesiastes leaves that question open (cf. 2:24f.). One can speak of God's gifts, but in the end all is vanity. Hosea holds out a God whose steadfast love will not be limited by human standards. Colossians asserts that our baptismal link to Christ's death and resurrection empowers us to strip off the clothing of the old way of living and to put on the fresh, and ever-refreshed clothing of the new creation in Christ that binds all things together in the perfect maturity defined by love.

That love teaches us that life is not controlled by those elemental principles that pass themselves off as true wisdom, but in the end are unmasked as counterfeit pretenders to the throne. Reason or wisdom has difficulty with hope because it sees things as they are (cf. Col. 3:10) or finds only false answers. It has difficulty in imagining what is not or has not yet come to be. That kind of wisdom comes from a knowledge that is continuously being recreated and renewed after the likeness of the one whose power has created all things.

That wisdom lies in a life that arises out of death by being united with the resurrection of our Lord. That is a life that is hidden with God in Christ who is indeed our life. And as Luke says, there is nothing hidden that will not be revealed (12:2). That revelation, when it comes, has to do with a life that is empowered by the Spirit and, so empowered, is enabled to store up riches toward God (12:21).

Twelfth Sunday after Pentecost
Nineteenth Sunday in Ordinary Time/Proper 14

Lectionary	First Lesson	Psalm	Second Lesson	Gospel
Revised Common	Gen. 15:1-6 or Isa. 1:1, 10-20	Ps. 33:12-22 or 50:1-8, 22-23	Heb. 11:1-3, 8-16	Luke 12:32-40
Episcopal (BCP)	Gen. 15:1-6	Psalm 33 or 33:12-15, 18-22	Heb. 11:1-3, (4-7), 8-16	Luke 12:32-40
Roman Catholic	Wisd. 18:6-9	Ps. 33:1, 12, 18-22	Heb. 11:1-2, 8-19 or 11:1-2, 8-12	Luke 12:32-48 or 12:35-40
Lutheran (LBW)	Gen. 15:1-6	Psalm 33	Heb. 11:1-3, 8-16	Luke 12:32-40

FIRST LESSON: GENESIS 15:1-6; WISDOM 18:6-9; ISAIAH 1:1, 10-20

Genesis 15:1-6. After Lot's rescue by Abram (Gen. 14:17-24) Melchizidek, king of Salem, arrives to bless Abram in words that are essentially a reversal of the traditional formula: instead of "Blessed be God" (*baruch Adonai*), we hear "Blessed be Abram (*baruch Abram*) by God most high."

Now this blessing is reconfirmed ("things" in "After these things" [1] comes from the root meaning "word") by the Lord directly in a vision. The first part of the promise—"I am your shield"—is passed over; it is the second part that is problematic, and Abram gets directly to the point. "Reward" implies posterity—a child. The "I" of God's shield is challenged by the "I" of Abram's pain at God's apparent forgetfulness: "What will you give me, since I continue childless?"

Before God can reply, Abram answers his own question: "apparently nothing," for the facts are "You have not given me a child." In the Hebrew, the "not" stands between "to me" and "you have given," as if to say the word of promise has not succeeded in bringing "child" and "me" together. That distance allows only one conclusion: "So" (lit. "behold," 3), since you have not given, other events will prevail. A "slave of *my house* is to be *my* heir." The promise is void.

Abram's conclusion is no conclusion. His "behold" is challenged by the Lord's new address. "Behold [in Hebrew; NRSV, "But"], the word of the Lord came to him." It mirrors the opening (cf. 1 and 4), but here underscores Abram's error. The first word (in Hebrew) the Lord speaks is a big "No" to Abram's construal, accenting the reversal by threefold repetition of "being heir." This man "Not! *will be heir*," but rather "one who will come from the body of you (the expansion makes the point) *will be heir*." In the literal text itself, and in what this text implies, the word of the Lord has power to change what is not into what will be—it is sheer promise!

Yet Abram apparently needs more. So the Lord "brings him out" for an object lesson. Just as God "brought" him out from Ur (cf. recollection of this in 15:7), God "brought" him out again for a "vision" (cf. 15:1) of a different sort. "Look" at the innumerable stars ("if you can count them," 5). So shall be your "offspring" (NRSV, "descendants") states the promise in words taken directly from Abram's own mouth (cf. 3). But whereas Abram could see only distance between himself and offspring ("to me *not* you gave offspring," 3) and the Lord as the direct cause of the failure ("not *you* gave"), now offspring and Abram are literally welded together by the Lord's promise: "So it shall be *your-offspring*" (in Hebrew the "your" is a pronominal suffix to "offspring" as one word). The promise is restated forcefully and simply, "it shall be so," its credibility resting solely on the one who speaks it.

But there is still more. Because Abram's "not" conceived "offspring" as "one," the lack of this singular child still stuck in his craw, God's promise leaps to "offspring" as innumerable as the stars of the heavens. God will act far beyond his wildest imagination. The promise is not just restated; God's promise is a plurality.

The conclusion is swift and spare, bearing witness to the power of the word. Immediately upon the promise (the last word in v. 5 is "your-offspring") the opening word of v. 6 is "And he believed." The word, preserved in our "Amen," suggests faithfulness, confirming, and establishing. Abram speaks an "Amen" to the Lord's promises; that "Amen" is "reckoned, regarded, deemed, considered" as righteousness.

In the context there is no need to search long and hard for the meaning of this "righteousness." It recalls the "blessing" spoken just before by Melchizedek, the king of "righteousness" (14:18). Here it refers to Abram's "Amen" to the assurance that his descendants will be as the Lord has promised. This reality is underscored in Hebrew by the "perfect" aspect of Abram's response that is paired with the "imperfect" aspect of the continuing "reckoning" of God. Abram's response has a completeness that is held fast in the ongoing reckoning of God.

God's ultimate responsibility is underscored in the subsequent divine pronouncement, "I am Yahweh, who brought you out to give you this land to possess" (7). But that the story of the promise is not yet over—we shall return for another day—is noted in Abram's response, "But how shall I know?" Possession remains the sticky point. It is the last word both of the Lord's promise, and of Abram's question.

Wisdom 18:6-9. The generally upbeat perspective of Wisdom and of this lesson is quite different from that of Ecclesiastes (see the Eleventh Sunday after Pentecost) in its conviction that wisdom is a gift of God's spirit and teaches the way of salvation and immortality:

1. Wisdom teaches God's people in advance to know the surety of God's promises so they might recognize their fulfillment when that occurs (18.6).

2. The perception of life is basically dualistic, balanced between salvation ("deliverance," 18:7; Greek *soteria*) for God's people and punishment ("destruction," 18:7; Greek *apoleia*; cf. the same pair in Phil. 1:28) for God's enemies. What for God's enemies is a sign of punishment or destruction, for God's people, taught by wisdom what to "expect" (18:7), is the working of God's glory (18:7-8).

3. Wisdom understands the "divine law," however hidden, that enables the "saints" even in the midst of suffering to know that all God's people will share alike in God's blessings, and thus to sing the praises of those who remain faithful (18:9).

Isaiah 1:1, 10-20. This reading from the beginning of Isaiah's prophecy grounds the crisis of Judah and Jerusalem similarly to Hosea (cf. the Tenth and Eleventh Sundays after Pentecost): God's children have "rebelled" and "do not know" and "do not understand" (1:2). The oracle is divided into two parts by the "word" of the Lord (*dabar*; 2, 10) and linked by the concluding reference to "rebellion" (2, 20) and its correlation of the people's prosperity or punishment with the faithful exercise of worship of Yahweh (cf. 11-17 to Amos 5:21-24). The first part (10-15) declares the utter wickedness of the people, the second (16-20) calls for repentance and renewal, holding out the promise of good fortune and restoration conditioned upon renewal of covenant obedience (19). The climax of the first section (15) is visually shocking when we realize that hands (actually "palms") stretched out in worship and prayer are actually full of blood.

The second section (16-20) holds out hope that these "scarlet" sins will be washed away in a repentance that ushers in ever-more specific good actions in a living "dialog" of God and people (17-18).

SECOND LESSON: HEBREWS 11:1-19

The epistle to the Hebrews is about *faith,* both in its recital of the faithfulness of God in the promises made real in the Son and in the corresponding call to a persevering faith of mutual encouragement in love (cf. 10:19, 23-34, 39). The "definition" of faith in 11:1 is surely one of the most familiar pieces of Scripture, and in some ways one of the most obscure to the modern reader. Its common translation in terms of personal "assurance" and "conviction" masks an underlying worldview that assumes what is "not seen" and only "hoped for" (cf. Rom. 8:24-25) is for that reason more real than this world of experience. By his incarnation Jesus bridges the gulf between that true heavenly realm and this shadowy earthly one, and by his death and resurrection he has become the pioneer of a new humanity that will follow its leader, abandoning the "tents" of this temporary sojourn in a "foreign" land (11:9) and arriving in a "city" that has *real* "foundations" because its "architect and builder is God" (11:10).

Two key words (NRSV: "assurance" and "conviction"; NIV: "being sure" and "being certain") define these "hoped for" and "not seen" things of faith. The first (*hypostasis*; only three times in Hebrews—1:3; 3:14; 11:1; and twice in 2 Corinthians—9:4; 11:17) "always denotes the 'reality' of God which stands contrasted with the corruptible, shadowy, and merely prototypical character of [this present] world" (H. Koester, *TDNT*, 8:587f.). Faith is that which makes real what is now only "hoped for" and "not seen."

The second word is poetic and mutually explanatory; its definition must not be pressed too closely. As a noun (*elenkos*) it occurs only once in the New Testament, but in numerous verbal uses it always refers to subjecting something or someone to "interrogation," to bring to light evidence that is otherwise not seen (cf. John 3:20, "exposed"). This then is faith: it makes real, brings from unreality to reality, the promises of God.

Such a reality cannot be achieved in words, but is witnessed only in the lives of those who have it and have demonstrated it. Hence the text moves immediately to witness and testimony. The underlying word is the same word as "martyr" and refers to the fact that the ancestors "were attested to" or "witnessed to" as examples "because of their faith" (11:3).

The ensuing elaborate testimony, marked by the repeated catchword *faith* (3, 4, 5, 6, 7, 8, 9, 11, 13, and so forth), begins from creation and focuses in Abraham as the premier example. Consistent with the definition of faith above, particular mention is made of his having been a sojourner in a land of "promise," heir to another "city" never attained, but seen only "from a distance" (10, 11, 13-16). Ultimately then, faith rests not on some inner assurance or conviction, but on the reality and "faithfulness" of the one who made the promise (11).

GOSPEL: LUKE 12:32-40, (41-48)

The Gospel focuses the call and promise of God in as clear and direct a statement as occurs in Scripture. If striving for the kingdom is the object of those who are "rich toward God" (21, 30-31), then it comes as overwhelming surprise that the kingdom is pure gift: "It is the Father's good pleasure to *give* you the kingdom."

Verse 32 is the heart and deserves some meditation. It begins with the command not to fear, literally "Stop being afraid!" Fear (an important word for Luke) is the opposite of faith: "Don't fear, only believe" (8:50). "Not fearing" is what happens when God breaks in to do a new thing as at the birth of Jesus, Savior, Messiah, and Lord. So in turn Zechariah (1:13), Mary (1:30), the shepherds (2:9, 10), and the called disciples (5:10) are told not to fear.

The ensuing diminutive "flock," joined with the adjective "little," heightens the sense of peril or risk. There is good reason for "lambs in the midst of wolves" (10:3) to fear. But that such dear little ones are the object of God's firm resolve gives the *reason* for not fearing: "because" it is the Father's "good pleasure." This is the same "Father" to whom this disciple community has been invited to pray (11:2, see the Tenth Sunday after Pentecost), who knows your every need (12:30). This is the same "good pleasure" (*eudokia*) of God announced by the angels to the shepherds (2:14). It is there when God speaks from the heavens at Jesus' baptism and empowering with the Spirit for ministry (3:22). As in Gal. 1:15 the word actually means to "make a decision": "The Father *has decided* to give you the kingdom." One dare not miss the message of resolve in this "decision" language. It is at the heart of Luke's Gospel message from beginning to end, and as sweet as the Christmas message: it is part of God's good pleasure that "today, for you, has been born a savior who is Christ the Lord. So stop being afraid" (2:10-11).

That resolve and gift have a way of transforming the lives of those who receive it. "Where your treasure is, there your heart will be also." For the "unfailing" treasure (33-34) is certainly the kingdom. That kingdom lies within the prerogative of the Father to give, and the Father has decided to give it. Some might take offense at the gift of this Jesus, but this gift will have no other way than to have your heart. You will not remain the same. To use economic images, you will have to get used to buying and selling in a different way. You will need skills quite different from those used to things wearing out daily and to money slipping through the fingers like water or sand. This gift is an object you can trust to be there when the chips are down (33-34).

The two parables that follow sketch in telling Lukan detail an image of those whose hearts are shaped by this treasure, this gift. Being "dressed for action" (35, literally "having one's loins girded"; the perfect tense suggests complete readiness) is an apocalyptic image for Luke (three of six NT occurrences) that symbolizes preparedness, just as does having one's "lamps" lit (six of fourteen occurrences; here present tense suggests "lit so as to *keep on* burning"). But preparedness for what? The text says "for waiting." But "waiting," too, is special (six of fourteen occurrences). It is the attitude of Simeon and those who await the "consolation" (*paraklesis*) and "redemption" of Jerusalem (2:25, 38). It is Jesus' "waiting" acceptance of sinners that arouses grumbling criticism (15:2). It is the expectant waiting for the kingdom of a Joseph of Aremathea just before the surprising Easter dawn (23:51). This is the dynamic waiting for the master to return that marks the imagery of the messianic wedding banquet (cf. 14:1f.; 22:16). Thus the "knocking" and the "opening door" are a sign of the coming of the kingdom, of "blessedness" for an expectant and ready disciple community.

But then comes the surprise. When the door opens for this waiting "servant" band (later told only to expect to do their duty without reward; 17:8), surprisingly, it is now the master who like a slave "dresses for action" (NRSV "fastens his belt" disguises the crucial use of the same verb in 12:35 and 37), causes them to "sit down to eat" (banquet!), and approaches (literally "comes to their side") and "serves" (*diakonia*) them. In the action of this master we discover what "dressed for action" means: being ready to serve, taking on the attitude of *diakonia*. But in the master's actions we also discover for a second time what it means to be servants with such a master. He comes not to be served but to serve (cf. 22:26-27, "it is not to be so with you") those to whom the Father has decided to give the kingdom, and if they wait in eager readiness for that gift, whenever it comes, early, middle, or late, they are truly "blessed" (12:38; cf. 6:20-22; 7:23; 10:23).

The second parable, while continuing the theme of readiness, introduces a surprising association. If the "owner" who is to be ready at "any hour" corresponds in some way to disciples "dressed for action," then the awaited "master" of the first parable now becomes an unexpected "thief" who comes to "break into" one's house. Perhaps this "thief" will come to "break in" to your world and take you by surprise. Perhaps the parable must not be pressed too literally and simply focused by the point that Jesus gives it: You must be ready; the Son of Man is coming, and it will be when you least expect it.

The longer reading (41-48) adds a third parable about a "faithful manager," in answer to Peter's question whether the previous parable (note singular) is for the disciples or everyone. The application to discipleship changes from "being ready or awake" to "faithfulness" and responsible "action." Far from sitting around, responsible waiting means to be about those duties entrusted by the master. It is a telling detail that the opposite of this action is not just to sit around doing nothing (inaction) but to seize the opportunity of the master's delay to "eat, drink, and get drunk" (cf. a less perverse master in 12:19) and to "beat up on the other slaves."

Knowing implies special responsibility (47), while to the one who does not know, punishment comes, but with a lighter sentence. "Is that fair?" we might ask. But what is talk of fairness for ones who have received what they did not deserve, a gift? "To whom much is given" calls us back to the promise of the kingdom (32). "To whom much is given, much is required." This is a kingdom that seeks disciples who, like their master, come not to be served, but to serve. And there will be an accounting.

Each of the lessons reflects on different aspects of what it means for us to receive God's promise and how that shapes the life of the believer. Responsible conformity between worship of God and the actions of daily life does not come easy, even for ones about whom the Gospel says the Father has made a decision. As for Abraham, God takes our "not reality" and lack of hope, and turns it into reality, not by some performance we achieve, but by sheer gift. God decides, and the power of that decision fits us in preparedness for service so that when the Master does come we will be found not beating up on our fellow slaves, but exercising that discipline of love and care to which responsible discipleship calls us.

Thirteenth Sunday after Pentecost
Twentieth Sunday in Ordinary Time/Proper 15

Lectionary	First Lesson	Psalm	Second Lesson	Gospel
Revised Common	Jer. 23:23-29 or Isa. 5:1-7	Psalm 82 or 80:1-2, 8-19	Heb. 11:29—12:2	Luke 12:49-56
Episcopal (BCP)	Jer. 23:23-29	Psalm 82	Heb. 12:1-7, (8-10), 11-14	Luke 12:49-56
Roman Catholic	Jer. 38:4-6, 8-10	Ps. 40:2-4, 14, 18	Heb. 12:1-4	Luke 12:49-53
Lutheran (LBW)	Jer. 23:23-29	Psalm 82	Heb. 12:1-13	Luke 12:49-53

FIRST LESSON: JEREMIAH 23:23-29; ISAIAH 5:1-7

Jeremiah 23:23-29. The lesson for this Sunday belongs to a section of oracles concerning the reigns of Josiah's successor Jehoikim (609–598 B.C.E.), his son Jehoichin (598 B.C.E.), and Zedekiah. The writing most likely stems from the time of Zedekiah, whose puppet monarchy of vacillation and court intrigue immediately preceded the fall of Judah to Babylon. 22:1—23:22 sets the background in Jeremiah's call upon the "house of the king" to "act with justice and righteousness" toward the "alien, the orphan, and the widow" and not to shed "innocent blood" (22:1-3). But since the kings have scattered and driven away God's people, God promises to restore a remnant and to raise up a "righteous branch," a true shepherd of salvation whose name will be "Yahweh is our righteousness" (23:1-8). Prophets, too, are castigated for the false and weak-livered "visions of their own minds." Their promises that all "will be well" stand in contrast to the stormy and wrathful "word of the Lord" with its power to "turn the people from their evil way" (23:9-22).

The refrain "says the Lord" (ten times in 23-32) joins the opening question, with its play on "nearby" and "far off," to assert that there is nowhere one can hide from God's presence or knowledge (23-24). In the end the "straw" dreams of the prophets will be consumed by the "fiery" word of Yahweh (28b-29).

At issue is Yahweh's "name" and those false "prophets" who fail to make it known faithfully. As v. 28a especially makes clear, Yahweh's "word" (*dabar*, used three times like a "trump" card at the climactic end of the passage) is contrasted with the mere "dreams" (five times in this lesson) of the false prophets. To underscore the distinction, the language describing their actions is appropriately differentiated. False prophets "tell" (*sepher*, 27, 28) their dreams; Yahweh's faithful "speak" (*dabar*! 28). Furthermore, the suffix "my" joined to verb and noun forms of *dabar* binds prophet, word of Yahweh, and Yahweh together as if symbolic of that prophetic faithfulness and unity. In fact, in the Hebrew, two occurrences of "word of me" surround "him" and his "speaking" just as the word of Yahweh surrounds and grounds the prophet in "faithfulness" and truth. In clear contrast, the false prophets do not proclaim in "official" language "an oracle of Yahweh"; they rather chant "*I* have dreamed, *I* have dreamed," their doubled first-person pronouncements seeking to disguise the fact that they have no further support than the false "I"s who propound them. Thus it is ironic when Yahweh credits them with prophesying lies "in my name," for that not even the text credits them with doing.

Here as elsewhere, the whole of Yahweh's character, reputation, and covenant relationship with the people is encompassed in Yahweh's "name." The prophets seek to drive a wedge between the people and Yahweh by causing them to "forget" the name of "Yahweh" and, like their ancestors, to substitute the "name" of Baal. Since their stories are merely deceitful dreams, they must bolster their stories by "telling" their dreams to one another; the "Word" of Yahweh stands on its own power and needs only to be "spoken" once by the faithful prophet.

In sum, the call is to faithful speaking of the "Word of Yahweh" grounded in Yahweh's "name," by which Yahweh is to be known as Israel's salvation and deliverer and as the wrathful God whose anger "like fire" will not turn away from those who deceitfully speak lies to God's people.

Isaiah 5:1-7. The deep expression of concern at Judah's desolation because of its arrogance and failure to match action with profession (cf. the Twelfth Sunday after Pentecost, Isaiah 1) sets the stage for one of the most moving poetic passages in the Scriptures, Yahweh's song of expectant love and concern for a dear planting, the people of Judah. The prophet begins singing indirectly on behalf of the lover: "Let *me* sing for *my* beloved *my* love song concerning *his* vineyard . . . *my* beloved" (1). The care for the vineyard and the intense expectation are suggested in the elaborate balanced description of its preparation. Yet the "expectation" (literally "he looked for") of grapes meets only a yield (*'asah*, "to do or make," see below) of wild grapes (2).

The intensity of expectation now overcomes the indirect third-person account; the Lord takes over the poet and poem to plead the Lord's case as plaintiff over against a wayward vineyard (3-4). Ironically, since the vineyard and "the inhabitants of Jerusalem and the people of Judah" are one, the juried hearers now sit in judgment on themselves (cf. 3 and 7).

The next unit (5-6) makes clear to whom judgment really belongs. The Lord retains "active" control over the situation as judge: "*I* will tell you what *I* will *do*" (cf. repetition of "do"; again *'asah*, 2, 4a, 4b). The first-person action is tantamount to "undoing" all the creative care exercised over the vineyard in the first unit (1-2). The vineyard will return to the chaos of briers and thorns; even the creation will participate in the abandonment: the clouds will not rain on it.

The final unit (7) establishes the "reason" for this extreme reversal. In a concentric arrangement, "vineyard" and "pleasant planting" form a frame surrounding the house of Israel and the people of Judah (7a), while the word *expected* (7b) recalls its counterpart at the end of each of the first two units. The "expectation" there unfulfilled in the "doing" of the vineyard now remains unmentioned. Two wordplays, by now among the most famous in the Old Testament, underscore the shocking reversal. The Lord looked for "justice," but *lo* "bloodshed" (*mishpat, mishpach*); (starkly with no connector) for "righteousness," but *lo* (note the parallism) a "cry of distress" (*zedakah, ze'akah*). In a theme recalled from the opening chapter (cf. 1:15), the paired expectation of Yahweh for "justice and righteousness" is unfulfilled in the reality of hands stained with blood.

The vivid poetry and the compelling rhetoric of this passage underscore the intense longing and pain of its content, and well account for its popularity. The appeal and theme continue in adaptation in the New Testament teaching of Jesus. The vine and branches (cf. John 15:1-11) are an image of the life of the Christian community. In the allegorical parable of the death of the Messiah, the wicked servants seek to appropriate the landowner's vineyard, killing the master's son, and throwing him outside the gate. The vineyard now becomes not only the direct object of the Lord's care and concern, but also the place for the working out of the divine drama of redemption, in response to which the community and the hearers are called to account.

SECOND LESSON: HEBREWS 11:29—12:2, (3-14)

The overall theme is an exhortation to God's "children" (cf. 12:5-11) to "endure" in the course set before them. The dynamic of that "endurance" (*hypomone*, six times in chaps. 10–12) is "faith," whose premier exemplars have been rehearsed at length (see the Twelfth Sunday after Pentecost) and are now gathered in a summary roll call ("Why should I speak at length. . . ?" 11:32). Such children know it to be part of God's plan that fulfillment of the promise must also include those of us who are even now being called to faithfulness and endurance according to the model and witness of those who have gone before (11:40).

Whether at the conclusion or the beginning of the reading, the huge "therefore" of 12:1 points to the climactic central argument of this section of Hebrews: Jesus is the ultimate model of faithfulness, who endured to the end so as to receive the promises of God.

The "cloud of witnesses" needs to be brought close precisely because the weight of "sin" seems so much more real because it "stands so close at hand" (*euperistatos*; a better translation than "clings so closely," 12:1). The Christian, however, lives in hope because faith enables "taking one's eyes off" what only seems so present and real and looking instead to the one who is made present and real only by faith: indeed, the very model of that endurance and faith, Jesus. Hebrews here calls him the "pioneer and perfecter" of faith, (*not* [!] "our" faith; there is no "our" in the text). That is, Jesus is the one who leads on before (*archegon*, "pioneer") and has already reached the end or goal (*teleiotes*) through *his* faithfulness. In the endurance of faith he despised the present-hand shamefulness and sin of the cross and looked beyond to the "joy that was set before him." So he has become our model in faith as well as the model of our hope in his resurrection and exaltation to sit at the right hand of God's throne of grace.

The continuation in Heb. 12:3-14 is focused by the question, If this is all true, then how does one in the midst of current trials still keep one's eyes confidently focused on the love, mercy, and promises of God? Several key answers are given: first, the reminder that everything that Jesus suffered was for your sake; second, that even if you suffer, your suffering is not to be compared with the suffering of Jesus, that is, to the point of "shedding blood" (4); and finally, the primary point, that suffering is a kind of "discipline" (*paideia*; seven times in 12:5-14 and only here in Hebrews) and the sign that we are indeed God's children. As by faith one is given to see beyond the present to a deeper level of experience and promise, so with discipline, what seems at the present a matter of "grief" rather than "joy," in the end "repays" or "renders" the fruit of righteousness and peace for those who have been "trained" by it to run the race that is set before them (12:11).

In light of this teaching, the final exhortation is to hang in there, to pick up drooping hands and paralyzed knees and run straight for the goal. The lame are to be so no longer, but rather to be healed so as not to turn from the course of the journey, and so to "pursue" that peace which is constituted in the eventual seeing of the Lord (12:14).

GOSPEL: LUKE 12:49-56

In the Greek the Gospel literally begins, "Fire I have come to cast on the earth." For the reader the effect is not unlike someone jumping up in a crowd and shouting "Fire!" The ordering of the words also deliberately connects "fire" with Jesus' "coming" and with the previous material about the "coming" of the master (see the Twelfth Sunday after Pentecost). Though the earlier sayings have focused on disciple preparedness, these two "I" sayings, unique to Luke, focus rather on the constraint that compels Jesus' ministry to its completion or "end" (*telos*, 50). Though "fire" is the attention-getter in the lesson, what is telling about this "coming" is this sense of goal. We move directly with the conjunction "and" to the language of "willing" or "wishing" (of hope) and of "constraint" or "compulsion" that links Jesus' coming directly to a "baptism" that has a proper "goal" or "end." This baptism (cf. Mark 10:38) will happen to, or be done to him. We are caught up in the sense of urgency and purpose in Jesus' words, but also caught up and held by a certain sense of a destiny that is beyond either his or our control. We are still, after all, "on the way" with one whose "face is set for Jerusalem."

The *telos* language invites comparison with Hebrews. Hebrews, too, makes much of Jesus as the "pioneer" and "perfecter" (*telos*, 12:2) in faithful suffering to the point of death on our behalf. If in our baptisms we are joined to the mission of Jesus, then one might well ask with the next section in what way this baptized community will experience the "end" or "goal" of the ministry of this one who has come "upon earth."

Whereas the preceding verses (49-50) are a tradition only in Luke, vv. 51-53 borrow from Q (cf. Matt. 10:34-36) and from apocalyptic "end time" material about divisions in families similar to Mic. 7:6. There, however, the division is a mark of the chaos and desolation of a wicked community under punishment. Here the division is occasioned by the "coming" of the Word of God and by the mission of "baptism" that moves to its fulfillment.

Thus it is clear that expectations about this coming—particularly false ones—need to be cleared up. "You are thinking," Jesus says (the original phrase may be either statement or question, as in the NRSV), that I have come to "give" peace. The effective change here from "casting" fire to "giving" peace (49, 51; the concluding phrase "on earth" invites the linking of the phrases) recalls the earlier reference to the Father's "giving" the kingdom (cf. 12:32; see the Twelfth Sunday after Pentecost). If the gift of God is the kingdom, then is not the arrival of the kingdom to be associated with peace, often the summary content of Jesus' mission and that of the early Christian community (cf. 1:79; 2:14,29; 7:50; 8:48; 10:5; 19:38; 24:36; Acts 9:31; 10:36)?

If you are thinking that the kingdom will simply mean the coming of peace on earth, you are wrong, Jesus says. What's more, his is not just a simple "no," but a strong assertion: "no way, not at all, absolutely not!" Peace and kingdom belong together, but the operative word is not peace, but "division," its importance emphasized through threefold repetition. This division into two camps (cf. "three against two and two against three," 52) is occasioned by the calling and decision of God that is offered in the giving of the kingdom to a disciple community. As this promise works its way into and through the world, the one whose life and death and mission is its occasion will also be the occasion of a division. The promise calls to responsibility. In a world not quite ready to hear that promise, that delights in the status quo, the "giving of the kingdom" and the "coming" of this word that is like "fire" will bring "division" in its call to discipleship that follows its Lord in mission. To be sure, the message will be peace; but this peace will have to do with salvation and hope for the downtrodden, the hopeless, and the marginalized of the world (cf. the songs of Mary, Zechariah, and Simeon in Luke 1:46-55; 1:68-79; and 2:29-32).

Whereas to this point Jesus' words have been addressed to Peter and the disciples (cf. 12.41), now he turns to the "crowds" (the text actually reads "said *also* to the crowds," not "*also* said to the crowds") with remarks unified by the theme of "seeing" and "judging" (*dokimazo*), a theme with which the term *hypocrites* also belongs (from the same Greek root as "judge," it literally means ones who are "acting a part" and thus making "false judgments").

The link with the previous sayings is more tenuous, but the context invites seeing this section as further reflection on the "coming" of Jesus and upon the expectations of those who either await or experience his coming. The link is made verbally by the explicit reference to "face of the *earth*" (occurring thus in each of the three units). In the reference to false judgment, connection is also made to the false expectations about "peace" and the kingdom, and perhaps even to the surprising "fire" to be associated with Jesus' coming.

The double image with its verbal parallels (54-55) underscores the accurate ability to "read" the signs of the earth and thus sets up the abrupt reversal of that judgment in the sudden "Hypocrites!" Knowing (three times in these verses) is thus contrasted with "not knowing" and pressed further in that this "knowing" has competence in superficial and earthly things (cf. 12:21, 34) but fails in that knowledge that has to do with making judgments about the "present time." The translation "time" here is both unfortunate and difficult, but crucial. The Greek word for time here (*kairos*) does not mean time as on a watch or calendar, but time that has to do with the critical or crucial times of judgment or decision; it is like "crisis." Thus this word, too, brings the reader precisely to the issue of decision, or division, and ultimately back to that most crucial decision of the Father to give the kingdom. That crucial decision is always present to divide those who receive and act on the gift from those who take offense at the gift and the sign and occasion of its fulfillment, the one who has come "to be baptized" and whose journey to Jerusalem is under constraint until it shall be fulfilled, both in Jesus' own life and mission and in the community of disciples who follow him on the way to Jerusalem and the cross.

Decision language is apparent in this passage. This call and this gift is not one to be set aside. As for Jeremiah, it drives to the division of true and false renderings of God's work of salvation. When the Word of God comes, it comes in power that challenges us to change. The key question is whether we will recognize that kingdom and its power when it comes, or will we still wait for another more favorable to our own delights and instincts.

Fourteenth Sunday after Pentecost
Twenty-First Sunday in Ordinary Time/Proper 16

Lectionary	First Lesson	Psalm	Second Lesson	Gospel
Revised Common	Isa. 58:9b-14 or Jer. 1:4-10	Ps. 103:1-8 or 71:1-6	Heb. 12:18-29	Luke 13:10-17
Episcopal (BCP)	Isa. 28:14-22	Psalm 46	Heb. 12:18-19, 22-29	Luke 13:22-30
Roman Catholic	Isa. 66:18-21	Ps. 117:1-2	Heb. 12:5-7, 11-13	Luke 13:22-30
Lutheran (LBW)	Isa. 66:18-23	Psalm 117	Heb. 12:18-24	Luke 13:22-30

FIRST LESSON: ISAIAH 58:9b-14; 66:18-23; JEREMIAH 1:4-10

Isaiah 58:9b-14. Chapter 58, concluding with an oracular pronouncement identifying the whole as a word of the Lord (14c), divides into three major sections, of which this reading forms the third:

> 1. Superficial/improper fasting—the Lord will not hear (1-5)
> 2. Proper fasting—the Lord will hear (6-9a)
> 3. Two if–then units
>   a. Social, action towards others (9b-12)
>   b. Worship, keeping the sabbath (13-14ab)

The first two units are bound together by the theme of Yahweh's hearing conditioned upon the proper "fasting" of the people. Proper fasting involves concern for injustice and oppression, sharing bread with the hungry, and providing clothing for the naked. Such fasting conditions a reopening of the lines of communication with Yahweh, whose responsiveness is confirmed by the use of the divine name: "Here I am" (6-9a).

The third unit now imitates the second in relating Yahweh's response to the people's proper action (Is this not? . . . then). Two subunits with similar formal structure specifically focus the conditional content in terms of social and personal relationships (9b-12) or "keeping the sabbath" (13-14ab).

Both of these subunits focus on the interrelationship of the promise and presence of Yahweh with the people's responsible action and worship. Just as failure to live with actions and profession in harmony has occasioned the captivity and exile, so now return from exile and restoration of the people and homeland depend on lives that bring worship and action, delight in the Lord, and actions on behalf of the needs of one another into responsible harmony.

Difficult in this passage is its conditional format. "If you do. . . , then Yahweh will. . . , you will. . . ." Are we to imagine the promises of the Lord dependent as reward upon people's initiative? To put it just so is not helpful. Better to say that authentic and true delight in Yahweh in worship and action occasions a mutual relationship of love and trust that belongs to God's people.

Isaiah 66:18-23. The key theme of this glorious conclusion of Isaiah's prophecy is an enduring restoration of Israel from captivity and exile to Jerusalem. The role of "surviving" Israel, gathered from every corner of the earth, is not to hoard this "sign" in their midst, but to be "sent" as emissaries with a particular story to tell, to "declare God's glory" (19). In a glorious vision all creation is restored to Zion. God's action in creation and the fortunes of Israel are conjoined as "all flesh" gathers before the Lord in worship (23).

With such a glorious closing note, it is not surprising that one should wish not to include the final verse of Isaiah, a reminder of the flip side of the coin. There is a minority report regarding those who will not be intrigued or drawn by the "glory" of Yahweh and who will persist in "rebellion" (24). Their rebellion has an "endless" story as well—not in worship but in torment and punishment.

These two words must stand together at the end of the vision. Even if the last verse is not read, it dare not be silenced by the selective task of reading in community. Certainly its note is consistent with the theology of Isaiah, that has linked punishment and exile with the rebellion of a faithless people and has argued that in the worship of Yahweh profession and action belong together for the restoration of all creation and all nations.

Jeremiah 1:4-10. This reading narrates Jeremiah's call (for Jeremiah's context, see the Thirteenth Sunday after Pentecost) in typical call-narrative fashion: (1) the call proper with announcement of the office/duty (vv. 4-5); (v. 2) the response of the hearer with excuses/rationale (v. 6); and (3) reassertion of the call with promise to be with, to deliver, and to empower the prophet, with further elaboration of the content of the message the prophet is commissioned to deliver (vv. 7-10).

Yahweh's call makes four assertions: I formed you, I knew you, I set you apart, I appointed you as prophet. The "before you were born" underscores the call as Yahweh's initiative, not as benediction or reward. Finally, that Jeremiah is to be "prophet to the nations" signals that God's interest goes beyond the narrow interests of Israel or Judah; it is for the sake of "all nations."

Jeremiah's response is short and to the point: I am young (only a child) and don't know how to speak. His "not-knowing" effectively contrasts the "knowing" of God's call; the Lord knows, but the prospective prophet does not. Then the Lord answers, rejecting the "youth" argument out of hand, and asserting a threefold series of commands with supporting rationale to counter the two meager objections of Jeremiah: I am sending you, therefore you shall go; I am commanding you, therefore you shall know what to speak; I am with you to deliver you, therefore you shall not be afraid. As if in anticipation of the prophet's task, the commands are sealed with a "says the Lord" (literally, "an oracle of the Lord").

In further expansion of the call and in answer to Jeremiah's objection, the call is sealed as Yahweh's word is physically placed in the prophet's mouth so that he may "know" what to speak. The mission to "nations and king-doms" will be threefold: to " pluck up and tear down," "to destroy and over-throw," and "to build and to plant," the first two pointing to the exercise of Yahweh's judgment, the last holding a sign of hope—new "planting" reversing the "plucking up."

SECOND LESSON: HEBREWS 12:18-29

(For Hebrews 12:5-7, 11-13, see the comments on Hebrews 12:1-14 in the Thirteenth Sunday after Pentecost.)
The reader has been encouraged not to "lose heart" (12:3) but to "endure" (10:36; 12:1) by faith (10:38, 39; 11:1) which makes present and real the object of Christian hope. Building on such hope in Jesus Christ as the seal that "the one who has promised is faithful" (10:23), today's reasoned argument has three sections:

> A. Not Mt. Sinai (18-21);
> B. But Mt. Zion, City of the Living God (22-24).
> C. Beware! Don't refuse the Kingdom (25-29).

Sections A and B are an elaborate comparison based on the theme of the "new covenant" in Christ (24), each section noting their respective objects of approach. Typical of Hebrews, the argument hinges on "degree" (how much more/less); on "old" and "new" (then/now); or especially on the assumption that "touchable" things are of less reality than things not seen, of heavenly origin. Mt. Sinai is something that can be touched (18-21); Mt. Zion, on the other hand, is a "heavenly" Jerusalem, a city of the "living God," an "assembly" (*ekklesia*) of those who have finished the race to its end (*telos*, 23; this is the correct literal meaning underlying the NRSV's "righteous made perfect"). There is something of a paradox here, the key to which is faith. Faith in one sense makes real and present that hope, so that one can say they have attained it. Yet the final consummation of that hope awaits the end of the journey. The end of the journey is certain in the congregation of the firstborn righteous ones who have already reached the goal. It is more certain in the promise of the new covenant that has been made real and sure in the blood of the mediator Jesus with which they have been sprinkled and sealed in their baptism.

In light of these assertions, section C again calls the community not to lose heart and fail in the journey, confident in the blood of Jesus (24) as that which calls and invites the community to faithfulness. At Sinai "then" the call shook the earth, but "now" a voice comes in a "once for all" promise of a shaking that will change or transform (NRSV "removal," *metathesis*) all of creation into the "unshakable" and enduring reality of the "kingdom." Here "city of the living God" and the "kingdom that cannot be shaken" have come together in content. This kingdom is not a sure and final possession. It still awaits the end of the journey. But it is this kingdom which we are in the continuous process of receiving that occasions the continuous thanksgiving (both present tenses) of worship that is acceptable to God.

GOSPEL: LUKE 13:10-17; 13:22-30

Luke 13:10-17. Last Sunday's Gospel ended with the call to recognize times of "decision" (*kairos*) when the word of God is present to accomplish its purpose. That seriousness about God's presence in every moment is reiterated in the next several units. Luke 12:57-59 speaks of making the crucial decisions necessary to avoid an irremediable punishment. Then, in a unique episode placed just prior to the parable of the fig tree and its challenge—"bear fruit or perish"—Jesus is pressed with questions about Galileans who have been killed by Pilate—right in the midst of their sacrifices.

Jesus avoids the implied question of the relationship of suffering and sin, and instead takes the occasion to issue a warning. The more important question for all is whether or not they will repent. Suffering awaits everybody who does not take seriously the need for repentance. The issue of suffering surely provides a link to this Sunday's Gospel narrative about a woman whose illness has extended over eighteen years.

The brief setting brings significant issues immediately to the fore. Jesus is "teacher"; he is in one of the "synagogues"; it is "on the sabbath." It is so characteristic of Jesus' ministry since its beginning at Nazareth (cf. 4:15, 16-30); we should be expecting that the moment is ripe for conflict. It will make good on Jesus' previous announcement that he came not to bring peace, but division. In his presence decisions are about to be occasioned and forthcoming.

The reading for the day can be divided into three units: (*a*) healing of a woman, a miracle story (11-13); (*b*) response to the healing by the "leader of the synagogue" (14); and (*c*) Jesus' response to the leader (15-17).

The healing narrative (*a*), however brief, has all the components of a typical miracle story: description of the illness (problem, 11); the healing proper (12); and the proof or corroboration of the healing (13). It begins cryptically, "And behold, a woman . . ." (NRSV is too wordy). She goes unnamed, but elaborate description of the illness stated first positively and then negatively highlights its extremity (and thus the wonder of the miracle): she is "bent" and not able to "unbend," and then finally, in case it is missed, an additional "completely" ends the clause (NRSV's "quite" avoids the effect of this complete finality).

"And/but beholds her Jesus"—so begins v. 12 mirroring the opening of the narrative. The first thing we hear is that Jesus sees her; then he "addresses" her (this more usual meaning for the verb is more fitting; not "calls her over" to himself, unusual for this verb, and besides she is crippled). Jesus makes the first move and speaks: Woman, "you have been set free from your paralysis." His speech signals power at work on several counts. The verb "set free" is from the same root as the verb "paralyzed." Hence, for her to be set free literally means to be removed from her paralysis. Second, the repetition of the same word for her "ailment" here and in v. 11 underscores that what she "had" at the beginning has now been completely removed (perfect tense of present reality). In Jesus' word what is promised has become reality for her. That Jesus further lays hands on her now binds word and action in a unit.

The proof of the miracle is a spare three words: "and she began to give glory/praise to God." The woman knows, as the reader is meant to, that this power she has experienced comes not just from this wandering prophet; it is a sign of the presence and blessing of God. She directs her praise appropriately. Further, the imperfect tense suggests a change of direction and livelihood that now only has its begining and will continue beyond the immediate narrative.

Those around, however, in particular the "leader of the synagogue," will not allow the story to continue in that unending praise of God. He wants to stop the "train" and derail it. He "answers" the event (the same verb describes the leader's response in 14 as that of Jesus in 15; they are intentionally parallel), and the imperfect tense of his action is continuously parallel to that of the woman: whereas she cannot stop giving glory to God, he cannot stop being "indignant," not at the healing, but because Jesus "healed on the sabbath." The woman knew where to direct her response;

the leader's response is directed neither to the woman nor to Jesus. He takes the sneaky, indirect approach and begins to harangue the nearby crowd with a sidewise swipe: "There are six days in the week on which to work, you people ought to come on one of them to be healed, and not on the day of the sabbath." As if healing is work, and as if the healing is done by them rather than by another (at least he gets the passive voice right: "to be healed"). It is as if to say, "Don't you people be like this woman!"

Jesus also "answers" (c), but whereas the leader's "answer" is scatter-shot, Jesus, now identified as Lord, speaks direct and to the point. The issue of the "sabbath" has stuck in the leader's craw. For him the sabbath is a big *not*: "Not on the sabbath day." For Jesus "on the sabbath day" is also the last word (16), but without a "not." The sabbath is "for" something, for releasing those in bondage, and what better object than this woman who has been in bondage to Satan for eighteen years, and who is, after all, one of the daughters of Abraham. There is an ironic direct challenge, missed in the translations (the same word is used for "untying" an ox or ass as for "setting free" from bondage), that underscores the "hypocrisy" and hard-ness of heart of the leader, who is willing to do for dumb animals what he is not willing to have happen to another who is like him a child of Abra-ham. To what lengths will people go to keep others in bondage?

The concluding verse (17) makes clear that the leader's bondage extends beyond himself. "All the opponents" are put to shame. The imper-fect verb again suggests a shame that begins and continues beyond this narrative. Their reaction to the healing has shut them out from the power and presence of God; their shame and bondage remains. The crowd, on the other hand, not duped by the leader's misleading, joins "entire/as a whole!" on the woman's side. They too are swept up and outside of the event with a joy that extends into the future. They began and went on rejoicing, and join the woman in directing praise or "glory" to God. In the reference to "wonderful things" (literally, "the things of glory"), glory is there in Jesus' healing, and glory still shines through at the end of the story. In his word and deed the "glory" of God was being unleashed, and for those who were released from bondage by its power, the only response is to rejoice.

This narrative makes clear that Jesus' ministry marks the coming of the kingdom that intends to break open the bondage to Satan. That the present reality of the kingdom is what is really at issue in this narrative of healing is underscored by the immediate link to the narrative that follows. Both by the sequence and by the linking word *therefore* the connection is made. It is as if to say, "If this is what 'happens' in the activity of this Jesus, then what are we to imagine that the kingdom is like?" This is not such a bad question even for those of us who claim to follow him as disciples in the present.

The story of the healing of the woman is telling. If the sabbath is a symbol of God's ownership of the world, of the exercise of God's power for delivering from bondage, then honoring the sabbath is connected with all those things that have to do with easing the yoke, feeding the hungry, speaking words of kindness. Will we recognize our identity in healing and joy with the woman, or will we take our side with the adversaries who have lots of sympathy for the beasts, but little affinity for unleashing the bonds of Satan in our world, wherever and whenever God's power is made known?

Luke 13:22-30. Talk of the kingdom is explicit in the narrative that follows. In vv. 19-21 a doubled question about the "kingdom" is answered by two parallel "comparisons"—like a mustard seed, like yeast—each by its very brevity calling attention to the surprising power of the kingdom when judged from its beginnings. The contrast with the next section (22-30) is thus dramatic, as is the intense weight of the subject matter. Mustard seed and yeast are rather homey; talk about "Who's going to be saved?" is getting down to brass tacks.

The transition is a strategic reminder of the journey of discipleship. For Jesus and for those who follow him the questions asked and the responses given are not just interesting excursions—the end of this journey is Jerusalem.

For Luke in a special way and for us caught up in this story the issue of discipleship is the issue of "salvation" (*sozo*, a little concordance work in Luke-Acts on this word is helpful). Salvation is at the center of the announcement to the shepherds: "For you today has been born, a *Savior*." There you have it, short and sweet. But is it really true? The framing of the question is telling of the mindset. Not how "many" are going to be saved, but rather how "few" is the locus of the fear. Has the message of the mustard seed and the yeast really not yet been heard?

As if to make matters worse, Jesus seems to turn the screws of fear even tighter. For him there is no, "Ease up, relax, it'll be OK." Rather, we hear of *one* narrow door, of many trying to get in with no avail, that some time ("when once," but who knows when? 25) the door will close excluding those left outside beating on the door.

If so, what can be trusted? We ate and drank with you and you taught in our streets. And what of the teaching itself? Did our ears deceive? "Knock, and it will be opened to you." There is no mistaking the answer from the other side of the door. Twice it comes. "I don't know where you come from!" (25, 27).

This is a troubling story. Whereas it clearly holds the reality of "salvation" (23) and "kingdom" together (28, 29), its description of entry into the kingdom as a matter of intense struggle ("strive," 24) is unsettling or at least puzzling. There are no easy answers; the only hint perhaps lies in the clear suggestion that exclusion in some way has to do with the "doing of injustice" (*adikia*, 27).

That the kingdom and salvation is serious business should have been clear in the recollection that this journey is with one who is on the way to Jerusalem and death. Some will be excluded. But one thing is sure, the speaker is not happy with the prospect, and the speaker has an answer to the original question. The issue is not "how few," but that "then" (29) there will be "so many"—and when they come from all the corners of the world and feast together in the kingdom of God, how sorry it will be if you who stand at the door are left out.

In our hearing we catch our breath on the edge of panic and long for a clear answer, a resolution. But all that comes is one more parable, another paradox. "Behold, some are last who will be first, and some are first who will be last." In the end if any are to be saved there is no secure way to make it happen. This word confirms that it is out of our control. It is, after all, God's kingdom. And who can stand to hear that kind of talk?

Not everyone, as the transition to the narrative immediately following reminds us. Some will simply want to do away with one who talks like this: "Herod wants to kill you" (31). Ultimately, it will only be those who do not take offense at this one who comes to die, those who are willing to surrender and be gathered like chicks in the tender mercy of God (34), those who can come to the time when we can say, "Blessed is the one who comes in the name of the Lord" (35).

Fifteenth Sunday after Pentecost
Twenty-Second Sunday in Ordinary Time/Proper 17

Lectionary	First Lesson	Psalm	Second Lesson	Gospel
Revised Common	Sir. 10:12-18 *or* Prov. 25:6-7 *or* Jer. 2:4-13	Psalm 112 *or* Ps. 81:1, 10-16	Heb. 13:1-8, 15-16	Luke 14:1, 7-14
Episcopal (BCP)	Sir. 10:(7-10),12-18	Psalm 112	Heb. 13:1-8	Luke 14:1, 7-14
Roman Catholic	Sir. 3:17-18, 20, 28-29	Ps. 68:4-7, 10-11	Heb. 12:18-19, 22-24a	Luke 14:1, 7-14
Lutheran (LBW)	Prov. 25:6-7	Psalm 112	Heb. 13:1-8	Luke 14:1, 7-14

FIRST LESSON: PROVERBS 25:6-7; SIRACH 3:17-29; 10:7-18; JEREMIAH 2:4-13

Each of the first lessons for this Sunday (with the exception of Jeremiah) come from "wisdom" traditions from the Old Testament and Apocrypha, each chosen for its theme of "humility," or its opposite, "arrogance," as a counterpart to the Gospel. They have a further common perspective about the nature and source of *true* wisdom (for Wisdom of Solomon and Ecclesiastes see notes on the Eleventh and Twelfth Sundays after Pentecost). Proverbs asserts that "the fear of the Lord is the beginning of wisdom" (9:10) and Sirach (the Wisdom of Ben Sira) echoes that belief: "All wisdom is from the Lord, and with him it remains forever" (1:1); "To fear the Lord is the beginning of wisdom" (1:14; cf. 1:16, 18, 20, 27). Wisdom is a mark of God's lavish grace "poured out" upon all creation (cf. Sir. 1:9).

Proverbs 25:6-7. Wisdom traditions are commonly associated with Solomon and attribute the great success of his early reign to his reliance on God for wisdom, and the corresponding decay of his later years to his departure from the "fear of the Lord."

These two short verses, coming from one of three collections identified as "Proverbs of Solomon" (1:1—9:18; 10:1—22:16; and 25:1—29:29), are chosen for the subject of "humility," though they are more likely linked loosely to the context by the common topic of "kings" and matters of "court." The first of the two-line sayings is synonymously parallel with a connecting "or." The move is from the more particular example—a "king"—to a more general one—"great people"—with roughly equivalent verbs—"put yourself forward," "stand." The second saying argues rather by comparison using the topic of "better and worse." Two features of "humility" are suggested, having to do with knowing one's place or station, and not stepping beyond that station inappropriately. Also present is the conviction that proper action according to wisdom holds within it the seeds of reward. To assume an improper station is to invite embarrassment or worse when told in the presence of superiors to move back where you belong. On the other hand, to assume a lower place is to invite the possibility that one's humility will be rewarded by the invitation to assume a place of more honor. Though not stated directly, the teaching holds out the promise that "virtue is its own reward." Though sounding somewhat self-serving or crass if taken out of context, we need to recall that the argument as always carries the conviction that relationships established correctly through wisdom are working themselves out according to the gift of God.

Sirach 3:17-29; 10:7-18. Whereas Proverbs associates its traditions with King Solomon, Ben Sira's fifty-one chapters, written sometime before 180 B.C.E. in Hebrew and translated by his grandson into Greek about 132 B.C.E, are steeped in devotion to the "Law" and the "Prophets" and the "other" writings as the sources of true and traditional wisdom. The conviction is that, by studying this wisdom, those who love learning will be enabled to live according to the "Torah" (see the Prologue to Sirach).

The first reading is joined to a collection on honoring one's parents (cf. 3:12). The "child" is now called upon to exercise humility in all "works" with an appended, twice-repeated promise of return or "finding favor" (17, 18; cf. the fourth commandment): "and you will be loved by those whom God accepts." Just as the fear of the Lord is the beginning of wisdom, so humility is recognizing the Lord's power and ascribing it appropriate glory (20). Humility also means to know one's own human station and limits and not to reach beyond what is appropriate to one's ability or gifts. This is not an invitation to ignorance but rather a recognition that some matters remain hidden from knowledge. As Sirach says, you have enough to do that is within your power; concentrate on those matters (21-24). The section concludes by contrasting those who are proud or "arrogant" and those who have wisdom or understanding (25-28). The arrogant have hard hearts and will end up piling sin upon sin for which there is no healing. The heart of the understanding, in contrast, is attentive to learning, with an ear that delights in proverbs (*parabole*). The associations with Jesus' teaching in "parables" and his call for those who have ears to hear is transparent, as are the connections of Jesus' teaching with wisdom traditions.

The reading from chap. 10 contains teaching about various types of persons or stations, especially those who are rulers or in high places. At the beginning of the section, "arrogance" (the word occurs four times in vv. 7-18) is identified with "injustice" and associated with wickedness. Arrogance stems from forgetting the identity and station that belongs to all by virtue of their humanity. Humility means remembrance that, after all, humans are but "dust" and "ashes." One can be a king today, but tomorrow may come death (9-10). Wisdom has a bit of reality consciousness about it.

More important is the recognition that arrogance or wickedness do not just happen. They have a root cause that goes much deeper. Just as the "fear of the Lord" is the "beginning" of wisdom, so wisdom now teaches that the "beginning" of arrogance is in "standing apart from," "forsaking" the Lord; it is the heart's abandoning of its creator, and, thereby, refusing to acknowledge its "status" as creation (12). Furthermore, the reading asserts, such abandonment of the Lord is "sin." Thus we have gotten to the nub of the issue. For wisdom the failure to acknowledge one's place and to live in humility without arrogance is in the end the result of "sin" (13). Sin (13) and injustice (7) belong together.

Just as humility will lead to the Lord's favor (3:18), so sin is the occasion of a deluge of punishments and destruction. In language recalled in the Magnificat of Luke 2, wisdom speaks of the reversals occasioned by the Lord: bringing down rulers and lifting up the lowly, rooting up nations and planting the humble, laying waste nations and erasing their memories from the earth (13b-17). Finally, wisdom returns to the theme of creation. Just as arrogance has its "beginning" in the forsaking of the one who is the "beginner," the "creator" (12), so it is true that "arrogance" was not part of God's intention for creation. The implication is that God's power will in the end act to root out arrogance from the human experience by utter destruction (18).

Jeremiah 2:4-13. In this Sunday's continuing reading we hear the central message Jeremiah is to proclaim in the form of a court trial in which Yahweh pleads before an imaginary judge. Verse 5 states the "facts" in a nutshell: your ancestors "went far" away in abandoning "me." The question is what wrongdoing on Yahweh's part was the occasion of such behavior, especially since the alternative choice was "worthless things."

This brief statement is then expanded in a carefully structured narrative of the basis for the charges. Two balanced units, each beginning with "They did not say, 'Where is the Lord?'" (6, 8), narrate in third-person distance the actions of those who rebelled against the Lord who sustained them in the wilderness in order to pursue "things that do not profit." The abandonment is total—priests, those skilled in law, the leaders, the prophets (6).

The "therefore" of the second unit (9-11) now brings the accusations directly. It is now no longer "they" who are in court but "you." Witnesses are called to join in adjudicating the absurd madness of this people who have chosen to do what no other nation has done—to change their gods to ones that are not gods at all.

In the final unit ("says the Lord," 12-13), the final summation is given while the whole creation is called to witness the enormity of a crime at which even the heavens will be shocked. Though ultimately God cannot let this people go—they are "my" people (cf. 11b, 13)—two evils mark their insanity. First, they have forsaken "me," the one who brought them out of Egypt into a land of plenty. Second, they have abandoned a good thing, "the fountain of living water," and have chosen to dig for themselves a cistern for stagnant water—and a leaky one at that! This last section is poetically rich with alliteration, word placement, and contrast: "water" that is "no water" forming a frame around "cisterns" that are "broken cisterns."

The message of Jeremiah does not disguise the deep sense of abandonment and hurt of Yahweh before the people of Israel. That sense is highlighted by the irony and sarcasm that underscores the ridiculous madness of a people whose choices are not in their own interest. The whole is set against the backdrop of an imaginary trial scene in which the hearers of the prophet and the readers of the prophecy are called upon to bear witness against "them," and then against themselves.

SECOND LESSON: HEBREWS 13:1-8, 15-16

(For Hebrews 12:18-24a, see the Fourteenth Sunday after Pentecost.)
The opening exhortation of Hebrews 13 is founded on the "therefore" of the gift of the "kingdom which cannot be shaken" (12:28) and ultimately on a chain of exhortation to "endurance" that extends back to 10:19 (see my remarks on the second lesson for the previous three Sundays).

A central proclamation underscores the conviction that Jesus Christ is the ultimate model of faith and that God is faithful in the promises: "Jesus Christ is the same yesterday and today and forever" (13:8). It is not surprising that this pithy affirmation should have been become a quotable quote to rival the one on faith from Heb. 11:1. But just as with faith, so this one risks misinterpretation if it is not linked closely to its context. This affirmation about Jesus Christ stands between two units, one with a series of traditional exhortations (cf. Rom. 12:9-21). The call is to exercise hospitality—love for one another, care for the sufferer and prisoner, honoring of marriage, contentment without greed—in the full confidence that God will not abandon them (13:1-5). Finally, they are to remember their leaders because (1) they have spoken the word, and (2) the course of their life has been worthy of imitation—particularly their "faith" (nicely the climactic final word in both the original and the NRSV, 13:7). It is this faith that leads to the affirmation about Jesus Christ, because (1) it is he who has been the sign and reality in the flesh of God's faithful promises, and (2) he is the supreme "leader" (*archegos*) and model of faith who has gone before.

This assertion about Jesus Christ now undergirds the argument of the unit that follows (13:9-16). Here the reading thus skips over a brief summary of the carefully reasoned argument that has occupied the whole last half of the letter. There the language of "sacrifice" (12:10, 15-16), "blood" (12:11-12), and "sin" (12:11); the somewhat allegorical treatment of Jesus' death "outside the gate of the camp" (12:11-13); and the reference to "seeking a city to come" (12:14), signal the old sacrificial system superseded by the once-for-all sacrifice of a new covenant in Jesus' death. Fully half of all the references to covenant in the New Testament (seventeen of thirty-three occurrences) are in Heb. 7:22—12:24. Jesus is "the same yesterday, today, and tomorrow" because he suffered for the sake of this new covenant promise, precisely in order to "sanctify a people through his own blood" (12:12; cf. 10:16-18, 29).

That Jesus is the "same" is the confession that ties together the assurance of hope (cf. 10:23) in this new covenant with a life of mutual encouragement and love that acts in the confidence that "the Lord is my helper" (12:6; cf. Ps. 118:6). Though this is no lasting city, there is yet one to come by the promise of God's grace. If 12:18-24 has suggested that we have in some way already arrived at this city (see the Fourteenth Sunday after Pentecost), then 13:14 balances this with its assertion that we are "continuing to look for" this city "which is yet to come." Thus Hebrews returns to its definition of the life of faith. Faith makes present and real to experience what in reality is only yet hoped for and not yet seen. It is that faith which enables finally the assertion that "through him" we offer the sacrifice of our actions of good deeds and mutual sharing (12:15-16).

GOSPEL: LUKE 14:1, 7-14

The setting for this narrative is crucial. In Herod's sinister threats (13:31) against a "prophet" who must not be "killed outside Jerusalem" (13:33), Jerusalem and death—the end of the journey of discipleship—begin to impinge ever so much more strongly on our reading and hearing. Again we are told that Jesus is doing something "on the sabbath" (cf. 13:10) and the Pharisees are "watching him closely" (cf. 6:7; 20:20). If the Son of Man is "Lord of the Sabbath," then more than the sabbath is on trial. They lie in wait anticipating his actions, knowing that his nature will be to do something offensive. They put to the test Jesus' own litmus: Who are the ones who can say, "Blessed is the one who comes in the name of the Lord" (13:35)?

The reading skips over the first of two stories joined here by this common introduction and setting, one addressing the issue of healing on the sabbath, the other on the subject of "places" (*topos*) at a banquet, only a slightly veiled allusion to the heavenly kingdom. Jesus "notices" the behavior of the guests (literally, "those invited," *kaleo*) and addresses a "parable" to them. In Lukan style the point is given along with this somewhat unusual "parable," in which the audience is addressed directly in exhortation characteristic of wisdom.

The reading may be divided into four parts: (1) address and occasion of the teaching (v. 7); (2) negative exhortation about choosing a place (vv. 8-9); (3) positive exhortation about choosing a place (vv. 10-11); and (4) exhortation about guest lists for banquets (vv. 12-14).

Several features are to be noted. Though ostensibly addressed to the guests, the consistent singular "you" and section 4's turn to the host and the subject of issuing invitations, make clear that for both hosts to the banquet and those who are invited as guests the whole is about the more all-encompassing issue of "banquets" and hence about the nature of the kingdom of heaven. A number of repeated words, mostly masked by translation, are helpful in getting a handle on this "parable." First, the repeated use of "place" (*topos*) focuses on who is "in" and who is "out" and on who has the power of "doorkeeper" over those who enter. Second, when Jesus warns guests not to choose places of "honor" (literally "first" [7, 8]), but rather to chose the "lowest" (literally the "last" places [9, 10]), we are quick to recall Jesus' earlier use of "first" and "last" as a key framework for talk about "salvation" and about who will be in the kingdom (13:30; see the Fourteenth Sunday after Pentecost).

The most telling vocabulary, however, is that of "call" and "blessing." The "guests" are literally "those who have been *called*" (7). For Luke, being "called" is central to discipleship and the kingdom. Fully half of the New Testament occurrences of the term are in Luke-Acts, and even in the Gospel the forty-three occurrences are almost twice the number in Matthew, the only close competitor. Jesus' instructions about invitations point to the "one who has called" ("host," 9, 10) and who is acknowledged to be in charge of the banquet. This language of "call," when joined to talk about "first" and "last," brings us squarely before a God who is about changing expectations and about unsettling surprises to the status quo (cf. the Magnificat, 1:46-55).

Thus, when Jesus finally turns to the host (the one who has "called"), the new standards for disciples are signaled in the language of "blessing" (*makarios*; cf. 6:20-22; 14:14-15). The etiquette of banqueting in the kingdom is not about expenditure and repayment, fair return on the dollar. It is about a "return" of a quite different sort. "You will be repaid," Jesus says, "at the resurrection of the dead" (14). Now *that* is a "return"! As surprising as the resurrection is the kind of "return" that this host has in store for you.

So when you "do" (*poieo*, this is "creation" language) a banquet, be creative, as God is creative (13). The word for banquet is literally a "welcoming," a "reception" (from *dechomai*). This banquet intends to "welcome" into its purview all those who are "called" by the one who issues the invitation. It recalls another grand "reception" and party thrown by Levi, another who experienced the "welcome" of God in Jesus' forgiving presence (5:29; see the Introduction). It is those who recognize their need of a physician who, when healed, also know how and why throwing parties is important and who know something about making guest lists appropriate to the kingdom. When you do a "reception," Jesus says, it is about inviting the "poor, the crippled, the lame, and the blind." The list is a duplicate of Jesus' address on that first day of his ministry and mission in the synagogue in Capernaum (4:16f.).

This is what salvation looks like. This story clearly asks this question to us as disciple communities called and sent with the mission to invite others to the banquet: How do we set priorities? Whom do we invite and in whose name do we imagine that the invitations are being extended? This is a great trust, but also a great tragedy, if we presume on our role as ones entrusted with the gospel, assuming that in the end we are the ones who issue the invitation and who set the standards for the banquet. We exercise our trust with a sense of gratitude for the blessing, with a sense that the "return" will always come each day as surprising as the Easter announcement—as unexpected and wonderful as the daily move from death to resurrection promised in baptism. Such discipleship is not goal-directed, but simply carrying out the mission of healing and salvation that is signaled in the cross of the one who journeys before.

Sixteenth Sunday after Pentecost
Twenty-Third Sunday in Ordinary Time/Proper 18

Lectionary	First Lesson	Psalm	Second Lesson	Gospel
Revised Common	Deut. 30:15-20 *or* Jer. 18:1-11	Psalm 1 *or* 139:1-6, 13-18	Philemon 1–21	Luke 14:25-33
Episcopal (BCP)	Deut. 30:15-20	Psalm 1	Philemon 1–20	Luke 14:25-33
Roman Catholic	Wisd. 9:13-18	Ps. 90:1, 3-6, 12-17	Philemon 9b–10, 12–17	Luke 14:25-33
Lutheran (LBW)	Prov. 9:8-12	Ps. 10:12-15, 17-19	Philemon 1, (2–9), 10–21	Luke 14:25-33

FIRST LESSON: DEUTERONOMY 30:15-20; PROVERBS 9:8-12; WISDOM 9:13-18; JEREMIAH 18:1-11

Deuteronomy 30:15-20. The first lesson belongs to the third of three addresses (1:6—4:40; 5–28; 29–30) in which, as the nation of Israel encamps on the plains of Moab prepared to enter the land of Canaan, Moses bids farewell, reciting the acts of God and calling for a renewal of covenant obedience. Although they "have seen all the Lord did" for them in the exodus and the wilderness, the Lord has not yet given them "a mind to understand, or eyes to see, or ears to hear" (29:2-4). Covenant obedience is the Lord's gift, and the promise is both for those now present and for "those who are not here with us today" (29:13-15). Covenant renewal anticipates a people again drawn to love the Lord because the word of promise is written on their heart (6, 14).

The lesson is divided into three sections presenting this call to obedience as the choice between "life" and "death"; obedience means to live in prosperity in the land of God's blessing, while its opposite is to perish and to forfeit the land:

A.   I have set before you today life . . . and death (15-16);
B.   I declare to you today . . . you shall perish (17-18);
A'.   Today I have set before you life and death: Choose life (19-20).

The verbal repetition of A', emphasizes the theme only explicitly stated in A': "Choose life." The direct address coupled with the "today" of all three sections underscores the seriousness of the choice to which the hearers are called. The issue is not to be put off until tomorrow.

The parallelism of "choices" in A and A' also provides expansion and variation on the theme: "life and prosperity, death and adversity" (A), but "life and death, blessings and curses" (A'). Life, prosperity, and blessing are further linked to covenant themes (cf. 30:6). Both A and A' set the basic theme of "loving the Lord your God" (16, 20), to which are added other paired themes: "walking in his ways" (A) balances "holding fast to him" (A'); "observing his commandments" (A) balances "obeying him" (A'). To all is added the promise of blessing in terms of life and the possession of the land that God has promised. "Then you shall live" (A) balances "for that means life" (A'); "God will bless you in the land" (A) balances "you may live in the land" (A').

These themes are set in relief by their contrasting negative counterparts in the middle section B. The alternative to not hearing/obeying is to forsake the Lord and bow down to other gods; the "promise" connected with this choice is that "you shall perish" and "not live" long "in the land."

This structure focuses clearly the call to the people to "choose" life instead of death. Typical of the Deuteronomic perspective and of the prophetic message (cf. Jeremiah below), life and prosperity are interdependent fruits of "loving the Lord your God, and walking in his ways," a call to obedience that the conclusion finally grounds in the continuation of the promises to Abraham.

Unfortunately, the NRSV makes more problematic this interrelation of promise and obedience by framing the opening call to choose in conditional terms and, thereby, obscuring obedience's dependence on the prior promise and activity of God. The NIV reflects much better the original's straightforward "I command you today. . . ," and "then you will live" (16). Clearly, even in obedience, the blessing still belongs to the Lord. The choice is whether to respond "by loving the Lord your God, and walking in his ways" so as to enter into the fruits that are "set before" those to whom God's gifts and promises are offered.

Proverbs 9:8-12. In Proverbs 8 and 9, personified Wisdom "calls" (8:1) the hearer to consider the rich benefits she has to offer. In Wisdom, first and foremost of God's creation (8:23), truth and righteousness reside (8:7-8); to listen to Wisdom and to walk in her ways is the foundation of happiness (8:32-34). Indeed, much as the choice is "set before" the hearer in Deut. 30:15, to find Wisdom is the decisive factor between life and death (8:35-36).

Chapter 9 forms three sections of six verses. In the two outside sections (1-6, 13-18), Wisdom and Folly issue their contrasting "calls"—Wisdom to a banquet of bread and wine that leads to maturity and life (5-6); Folly to "stolen water" and "secret bread" that stealthily leads to death and the depths of Sheol (17-18).

In the central six verses to which the reading belongs(7-12), a series of proverbial statements on wisdom differentiate their respective offerings and their appeal to the alternative respondents, the "scoffer" and the "wise." The wise and righteous person (here equated) profits from instruction, while the scoffer only retaliates against instruction with hatred and abuse (8-9). Wisdom further promises the benefit of long life and good fortune (11). In the end the choice of wisdom or folly is a matter of one's own responsibility (12).

In the very center stands the pivotal ground for the whole of this chapter and indeed of Proverbs' entire wisdom teaching: "The fear of the Lord is the beginning of wisdom." (10; cf. Job 28:28; Ps. 111:10; Prov. 1:7; 2:5; 14:26-27; 15:33; 19:23; 22:4). Wisdom is ultimately the Lord's possession and wisdom means to live by the word and promises of God's Torah. Wisdom and knowing the Lord are merged into one reality in which all of God's gifts are contained. Where there is wisdom, that is, the fear of the Lord, there is life and salvation.

Wisdom 9:13-18. This reading comes from the last portion of "Solomon's" prayer for wisdom in 9:1-18, reflecting the theme of wisdom as, above all, God's gift (8:21). The reading may be divided into two parts (13-16 and 17-18), each beginning with a variation on the question, Who can learn the counsel of God? In response to the first section's discouragement at the difficulty of "earthly" humans to track the matters of heaven, the second section in a fascinating way joins wisdom and the Spirit and identifies them as the gift of God enabling humans to search out and understand the will and counsel of God. If God seems inaccessible, then wisdom and the Holy Spirit are the gift of God to mediate God's will and purpose.

Two specific results of this gift are noted: (1) by wisdom and the Spirit the "paths" of humans are set straight, and they are taught the things that are pleasing to God; and (2) Wisdom is the agency of God's "salvation" ("by wisdom *they were saved*," 18). The emphasis on the gift of God, the sending of the Spirit, and salvation are instructive for New Testament comparisons (cf. Eph. 2:5, "by grace *you have been saved*"). What for the New Testament comes through the death and resurrection of Jesus Christ, and for Deuteronomy rests in the promise of the covenant, for Wisdom and Proverbs is anchored in the gift of wisdom.

Jeremiah 18:1-11. In the continuous reading from Jeremiah, the "word of the Lord" comes to Jeremiah again in the form of an object lesson (see the Thirteenth Sunday after Pentecost) carried out in parable-action by Jeremiah. The reading may be divided into four parts: (1) address and commission (vv. 1-2); (2) object lesson at the potter's house (vv. 3-6); (3) expansion on God's right to "change the mind, repent" (vv. 7-10); and (4) concluding oracle (v. 11).

In the first two sections, the potter's ability to reshape or completely rework the clay (cf. Isa. 45:9; Job 33:6; Rom. 9:20) is applied to God's relationship to Israel, the theme reinforced by concrete words for working, making, doing, and shaping, and by the link of potter's "house" to the house of Israel.

In section 3, in two balanced constructions, "at one moment . . . at another moment" (7, 9), God asserts that a prior divine declaration can be altered or changed (repented; cf. Exod. 32:12, 14; Jer. 26:3, 13; 36:3; Jon. 3:8-11; Job 42:6), conditioned upon the action or response of a nation or kingdom. God can change from intended "disaster" if the nation turns from evil; God can also change from intended "good" if the nation does evil.

The concluding oracle, addressed directly to Judah, brings the point home, by combining the image of the potter with the possibility that God may change God's mind from intended disaster contingent on the response of the people. If one breaks off the reading at v. 11, its ending call to repentance and amending of ways seems to leave open the possibility that God may indeed change the intended disaster. But the very next verse plunges from the heights of possibility to the depths of despair. "But they say, 'It is no use! We will follow our own plans, and each of us will act according to the stubbornness of our evil will.'" The choice is for evil and disaster.

SECOND LESSON: PHILEMON 1–21

Onesimus, a runaway slave, has come to Paul in prison. Now Paul returns the slave to his owner with this pastoral cover letter, adapting the conventions of letter-writing (Salutation/Greeting: 1–3; Thanksgiving: 4–7; Body: 8–19; Exhortation: 20–21; Closing/Benediction: 22–25), by effective use of language and argument to ward off any rash punishment ("my child," 10; "welcome him . . . as me," 17), and to assist Philemon in choosing to do the thing which is "good" (cf. 6, 14, 21). From first to last word, the argument is artfully cemented by puns, wordplays, and calculated repetitions (many difficult to see in translation). While Paul's second word calls for sympathetic response to his being a "prisoner" for the sake of Christ, for Philemon the whole letter is framed with the reminder that he is the recipient of God's grace in the Lord Jesus Christ (3, 25). The letter's address also "to the church in your home" reminds Philemon of his responsibility as a leader and that his choice and action will be public.

The thanksgiving expresses Paul's continual thanks that Philemon possesses the two cardinal virtues, love and faith (NRSV reverses the original in which each is chiastically related respectively to all the saints and to the Lord Jesus), and further prays, in anticipation of the main topic of the letter, that Philemon will be energized ("effective") in doing (literally "knowledge") of the "good" for Christ (6). In this way and by reference to Philemon's "encouragement" (*paraklesis*) and "refreshment" of the "hearts" of the saints, Paul sets up themes to be recalled in the body: the identification of Onesimus as Paul's own "heart" (12) that needs being "refreshed in Christ" (20); and Paul's desire to allow Philemon's "good deed" to be "voluntary" and not "forced" (14).

When Paul gets to the topic at hand, the name of Onesimus is delayed until the last possible moment (8–10) by a convoluted introduction in which he begins by saying "please" (*paraklesis*, 9) rather than by "commanding," and, by the way he reminds Philemon that he is after all *Paul*, an old man, and above all (once more) a prisoner—for Christ! Then even the name is broached amid Paul's wit. Anticipated by the statement that Paul's appeal comes "on behalf of my child whom I have fathered in prison" (the NRSV reverses the word order; imagine the wheels turning in Philemon's mind at this point!), the mention of the name is followed immediately by a clever pun on Onesimus, which means "useful" in Greek. The joke is clearly intended to relieve the tension and anger of the recipient, as is Paul's following reminder that he is respecting Philemon's maturity, faith, and love by not taking the matter of doing the "good" out of his hands.

In perhaps the most cleverly and artfully argued section of the letter (15–19), Paul anticipates in turn each of Philemon's protestations: Your loss was for an "instant"; your gain "for eternity." You lost a "slave"; you get back a "brother." If you can't stand him, pretend he is me, your partner. If he has wronged you in some minuscule way (the NRSV "in any way" represents the Greek word *ti*, the smallest word in the language!), Paul says, charge it to my account, and then literally writes an IOU, followed by the clever conclusion, "I won't even mention the fact that you owe me your whole life" (19). What rebuttal is left to Philemon?

When Paul now turns to the exhortation (20), it is by contrast as abstract and as indirect as the previous argument has been particular and direct. "Let me have some benefit from you" is once more a play on Onesimus's name (Greek *oninemi*, "beneficial," "useful"), and the reference to "refreshing my heart" calls for Philemon to do now in Paul's case what he has already shown himself good at for all the rest of the saints (cf. 7). Paul is calling in his chips, so to speak. As the crowning indirect request, which has, of course, never been specifically made, Paul says, "I know that you will do even more than I could ever ask" (21).

End of argument and exhortation? Only apparently, for in the conclusion (22) Paul adds the final clincher: "By the way, I will be coming to visit soon, so get a room ready. And remember, my coming will be God's gracious response to your own prayers for my release" (NRSV "restored" translates *charizomai, charis*). Then comes one final reminder, in case

Philemon has forgotten, that Paul who writes is "in prison" after all, and that the grace of the Lord Jesus Christ is with Philemon and the church at his house—the "your" (25) is plural.

GOSPEL: LUKE 14:25-33

The Gospel lesson is a carefully crafted collection of sayings of Jesus unified by a simple yet balanced structure (cf. D. Tiede, *Luke*, ACNT, p. 269):

26	Saying # 1:	If one comes to me and does not hate . . . is not able to be my disciple
27	Saying # 2:	If one does not bear cross and come after me . . . is not able to be my disciple
28-30	Illustration:	Cost of building a tower (you; agriculture)
31-32	Illustration:	Cost of going to war (king; military)
33	Conclusion:	If one does not say goodbye to all . . . is not able to be my disciple.

The thrice-repeated phrase, "is not able to be my disciple," (26, 27, 33), each time set as the concluding refrain of its clause (the NRSV reverses and rephrases the clause slightly; cf. the NIV), bears witness both to the structure and to the theme of the whole—discipleship or following Jesus. This theme is further prepared for in the brief setting reminding the reader of the "journey" to Jerusalem (see the Introduction) and is suggested in Jesus' address to the "many crowds," potential disciples, who are both invited and warned about "sitting down and estimating the cost" (28) of discipleship. It is further explicit in the characteristic discipleship vocabulary, "comes to [after] me," that chiastically frames the two conditional clauses of the first two sayings.

Two central requisites of discipleship are set side by side: hating one's relatives and even one's own life (the *eti te kai* effectively marks this clause in bold), and taking up the cross. The Greek present tense of all the verbs (26, 27, 33) underscores that this is no chance venture, but a commitment for the duration. Luke states the demand as radically as possible (not softening it as does Matt. 10:37f., where the radical hating and explicit language of "following" are missing).

The "costly" language is followed by two illustrations that speak of the need to count the cost of discipleship so as to be able to bring to completion (*telos*) a venture begun. If it is incumbent on those who deal with two important this-worldly enterprises—agriculture and politics—to plan carefully, then how much more for ones who respond to Jesus' call to follow him. This life-demanding and life-altering decision is the focus of the conclusion ("So therefore," 33) that draws the argument together. The verb translated as "give up" actually means to "say goodbye to" and refers to all that "belongs to one." The present tense again reminds that this "goodbye" is a radical disciple life chosen for the duration. On this journey with Jesus there will be no looking back (cf. 9:57-62).

The attached sayings on salt and hearing (34-35) are integral to this section on discipleship. The saying on "hearing" issues the call to discipleship to the reader, not withstanding its radical character. The danger for today's hearer, as for Luke's own community, is to be so awed and discouraged by the enormity of the call as to sidestep it, either by turning away in offense, or by softening its seemingly impossible demands. Yet Jesus holds out the promise that hearing and following are indeed possible, for it is the one who is journeying to Jerusalem and to the cross who invites hearers to "come after" him (9:18-24). This is the same one who announced that it is the Father's good pleasure (decision) to give the kingdom (12:32) and who, as resurrected Lord, commissions a disciple community empowered by the gift of God's Spirit (24:49). It is they who have been exposed to the sowing of the seed and who hold the promise of being the good soil that will hear the word and hold it fast with an honest and good heart (cf. 8:8, 15).

All of the lessons balance the wisdom of human life and the possibility of good and bad choices with the actions and purposes of God. The suggestion is clear that better or worse human choices are possible and that choices can and do make a difference in what God purposes and brings to fruition. This kind of talk of course raises red flags for a theology of grace that wishes to make sure its assertion that God is in control. These texts do not deny that assertion, but neither will they surrender human responsibility for the sake of preserving a place for the rights of God. God is still the potter, the author of wisdom, and the wisdom to make good choices is still the gift of God.

Seventeenth Sunday after Pentecost
Twenty-Fourth Sunday in Ordinary Time/Proper 19

Lectionary	First Lesson	Psalm	Second Lesson	Gospel
Revised Common	Exod. 32:7-14 or Jer. 4:11-12, 22-28	Ps. 51:1-10 or Psalm 14	I Tim. 1:12-17	Luke 15:1-10
Episcopal (BCP)	Exod. 32:1, 7-14	Ps. 51:1-8 or 51:1-11	I Tim. 1:12-17	Luke 15:1-10
Roman Catholic	Exod. 32:7-11,13-14	Ps. 51:3-4, 12-13, 15, 17-19	I Tim. 1:12-17	Luke 15:1-32 or 15:1-10
Lutheran (LBW)	Exod. 32:7-14	Ps. 51:1-18	I Tim. 1:12-17	Luke 15:1-10

FIRST LESSON: EXODUS 32:1, 7-14; JEREMIAH 4:11-12, 22-28

Exodus 32:1, 7-14. The infamous incident of the golden calf and the crisis between God, Moses and Aaron, and the people of Israel picks up with the Lord's announcement to Moses of what has happened while he has been up on the mountain to receive law. Verses 7-8 essentially repeat the content of v. 1, while the specific narrative of the "perverse actions" of the people—the making of the calf and the altar, and the offering of sacrifices—is included only by indirect reference.

God's opening words, "brought up out of the land of Egypt," is a theme heard already twice before (1, 4), and to be heard at least three more times (8, 11, 12). The repetition keeps in suspense two related issues: (1) to whom this perverse people belongs, and (2) who would claim to have "brought them up out of Egypt." The options are trotted out. First it was Moses "who brought," but now he's off who knows where. So now it is "these gods of yours" (the golden calf) who take Moses' place and become the object of worship. Even in revering Moses as their deliverer the people had forgotten the Lord.

Finally, even God will not claim them. It is "your people" whom "you" brought out who have acted so perversely. Their chant, "These are your gods who brought . . ." is proof of their abandonment of God. God is ready to abandon them as well: "Let me alone so my wrath can burn against them and consume them"(10).

But Moses intercedes, precisely by using God's own words on behalf of the people. They are "your people whom 'you' brought up out of the land." Moses cleverly argues that even the Egyptians know the truth—it is indeed God who has "brought them out"—and they will use this knowledge to ridicule God's intentions (12). Why should the Egyptians be able to turn God's actions into mockery? God's reputation as much as the people's is at stake.

Moses' intercession focuses on three words: "repent" (*shuv*) from your wrath; "change your mind" (*nacham*; see comments on Jeremiah 18 in the Sixteenth Sunday after Pentecost) about the intended disaster; and "remember" (*zachar*) the covenant you swore to your servants Abraham, Isaac, and Israel (12-13). It is a risky and bold intercession, but Moses will not let God escape the covenant. No matter how bad they may be, they are after all "your" people. You brought them out of the land of Egypt, and you have bound yourself to them with an oath sworn on your own self (13) that you would multiply them and give to their descendants the land (cf. Gen. 12:7; 15:5; 22:17).

The ensuing narrative of God's response bears witness to the effectiveness of Moses' intercession. Verbal repetition signals the congruence between intercession and response. "Change your mind [from the] disaster on the people of you" (12) parallels "And changed the mind the Lord from the disaster . . . on the people of him" (14). Significantly, the one change from verbatim response, from "your" to "his" people, confirms that in God's "change of mind" the people have been reclaimed as God's own. In one final touch, the word that describes what God has intended "to do" (*asar*, NRSV "to bring on") to the people, used repeatedly (1, 4, 8, 10) in the narrative to refer to the "casting" of the calf, and to God's "making" of a new people to replace this perverse one, now is instrumental in the reversal of the people's abandonment of God and in God's reclamation of the people through return to the commitment of the covenant promise.

Jeremiah 4:11-12, 22-28. The alternative reading from Jeremiah ends with exactly the same verb as has occupied the reading from Exodus, but at precisely the opposite place. Here God will *not* "change the mind" or turn back from bringing judgment and destruction upon the people of Judah (28).

In vivid and fearsome images, Jeremiah describes the destructive "hot wind" from the north (11) that will come in response to the people's wretched forsaking of God's sanctuary and their "whoring" after other gods on the mountain heights (1:16; 2:33—3:2), *because* the people are foolish and stupid and have chosen evil in place of good (19-22).

The concluding verses (23-28) imagine a wasteland devoid of living creatures, plants, and all cities of habitation, where even the heavenly lights have vanished and the mountains and hills no longer keep their foundations. The prospect is of an earth returned to a time before creation, to a state without God's creative hand, as if in reminder of the importance of God's sustaining mercy and love that the people have forgotten. Then the whole earth will be dressed in the black of mourning (28).

Yet, however small, the prophetic oracle holds out a word of hope: "Yet I will not make a full end" (27). God will not abandon the people completely.

SECOND LESSON: I TIMOTHY 1:12-17

The second lesson begins six Sundays of readings from 1 and 2 Timothy, traditionally included among the "Pastorals" along with Titus, because of their advice on matters of the life of faith and order within the Christian church. Though some regard Pauline authorship as problematic because of vocabulary, style, and the setting of the church represented, the letters certainly stand within Pauline tradition in their focus on the gospel in themes of faith, hope, and love.

The immediate concerns are sound teaching that leads to "sincere faith" and "love" that flows from a "pure heart" in the face of heterodox teachings and endless speculations (4) that threaten God's "economy" or "way of working" (better than the NRSV's "divine training") exercised through faith. Grounding in such faith ("trust") *is* the "sound teaching" that accords with the "glorious gospel" of God with which Paul has been "entrusted" (10-11). This "faith/entrusting" (the word means both) oscillates as the theme of the opening chapter. Including its application to the "genuinely faithful" Timothy, the word is used eleven times (2, 4, 5, 11, 12, 13, 14, 15, 16, and 19 twice). Such "faith" defines the experience of the gospel in our life and occasions the "thanksgiving" to which having been "faithed" or "entrusted" now leads.

In today's reading Paul gives "thanks" that the "grace" (both *charis*, 12, 14) of Christ has "overflowed" (literally, "hyper-increased") in "faith and love" that come from being "in Christ Jesus" (14; five more times in this letter faith and love are linked—1:5; 2:15; 4:12; 6:10, 11). "Faith" in this active sense of belief in Christ depends on the transition from v. 13 to v. 14, where "unfaith" is literally transformed into "faith" (*apistia* to *pistis*). Thus faith and love as present experience are dependent (in content and in order of thought in the text) on the prior experience of having been "regarded" as "faithful" (NRSV "judged"; for the same word see Phil. 2:5: "did not *regard* equality as a thing to be grasped"). Such new "regard" by Christ Jesus "empowered" Paul through his "appointment" for "service" (*diakonia*).

"But I received mercy." Twice this reality (the aorist passive underscores the complete and powerful transformation) is stated as the key to Paul's life of faith, each time coming immediately upon the description of the situation this mercy has transformed: "even though I was a blasphemer, a persecutor, and a man of violence" (13); "sinners of whom I am the foremost" (16). Thus "mercy" stands at the center of the two movements or divisions of the reading (12-14; 15-17), just as it stands at the *center* of grace and peace in the opening greeting (2).

The very first and linking word between the two sections is "faithful." "*Faithful* is the *saying* (*logos*) and of full acceptance *worthy*" (15; so the

Greek order; note the concentric framing of "word" by "faithful" and "worthy" at the extremes of the clause). The language is creedal, moving in the next phrase to state the central content of the "faith" to be taught. The creed has two parts: (1) a general statement of the "faithful *logos*"—Christ Jesus came into the world to save sinners" (15; note here and in v. 16's "eternal life" the similarities to John 3:16-17); and (2) personal testimony. Paul says, I have been shown mercy so that Christ Jesus might make me an example for all those who will come to faith in him. At this point creedal truth and personal experience come together and resolve in praise as "life eternal" (*aionios*) is redirected and verbally linked to its source, the king of the "ages" (*aionon*), to whom honor and glory belong "forever and ever" (*aionas ton aionon*). The reading ends where it began—from thanksgiving to doxology. The only fitting response is "Amen!"

GOSPEL: LUKE 15:1-10, (11-32)

Paul's experience of God's mercy in Christ for sinners is one way of expressing the heart of the gospel. The series of beloved parables of Luke 15 also expresses the depths of God's mercy and love for those who are lost.

Jesus' teaching from last Sunday (see the Sixteenth Sunday after Pentecost) concluded with the call to "salty" discipleship: "Let whoever has ears to hear, hear" (14:35). Now it is the last persons one would expect, those whom we might consider tasteless and fit only for the manure pile, who are indeed the ones who draw near to "listen" to Jesus. The description in the present linear that promises in this "listening" an openness to "continue" as a hearer is again a subtle reminder of the journey of Jesus and of the end toward which such discipleship will lead.

Though there has been no mention of a meal, the Pharisees and scribes cannot forget what it is they don't like about this Jesus. He has a habit of receiving sinners and eating with them. This story recalls many details of the very similar story of the banquet at Levi's house (5:29-32). Jesus hasn't changed his spots and what intensifies the grumbling now (5:30 with a *dia*- added) is that he is not likely to change them in the future (as is literally confirmed and fulfilled in the Zacchaeus episode at the end of the "journey," 19:1-10). Jesus' remark there, "I have come to call not the righteous but sinners to repentance" (5:32), is a backdrop for hearing this story, in which talk of "sinners" and "repentance" figure prominently again. What is different is that, whereas in the earlier story the image of Jesus was that of physician who comes to heal the "sick," here it is that of "seeker" who goes in search of the "lost."

In response to the "grumbling" Jesus told them "this parable." The singular "parable" makes clear that the whole of chap. 15—the lost sheep, the lost coin, and the lost son, as they are specifically described—are three parts of one parable teaching to be read in tandem. This is particularly true of the longer reading of the prodigal son and his brother, so rich with images and meanings that it is often treated as if standing alone.

This is more readily seen in the case of the first two parts, the lost sheep and the lost coin, whose structures and vocabulary are essentially parallel. The doubling of the stories, one with "a man," the other with "a woman," intensifies and universalizes them for all people. The numbers (one of one hundred, and one of ten) may be significant due to symbolism of the number ten, but are for the most part consistent to the particular situations described. More significant features are the following: (1) each "continues to pursue/search after" (the verbs are present tense) until the "lost" is found, suggesting that this behavior on the part of God is not likely to change any more than it has for Jesus thus far; (2) the "joy" expressed at the finding of the lost; (3) neighbors and friends are compelled to "rejoice" along with, implying that the joy is to spread to a broader community, to transform and fill all its surroundings, to be contagious; and (4) that such joy will exist (v. 7) and will continue (v. 10) in heaven/in the presence of the angels. All this points to divine purpose and mission as reflected in the ministry and journey of Jesus.

Two brief comments on the text: v. 7 should *not* read "*more joy* in heaven over . . ." but rather "there will be joy in heaven over one sinner who repents *rather than* over ninety-nine righteous who need no repentance." Second, the last phrase is not meant to suggest that righteous people do not need to repent, but rather that the righteous are those "sheep" already in the fold, who thereby show that they are already living by repentance.

The third part of "this" parable, the man with two sons, is an esthetically pleasing and masterful counterpart of the whole. Alongside stories of "a" man, and "a" woman, is set this story of "a" man with two sons. The ante is upped: two sons, one lost, one not, invite a ready comparison between the two. Aside from the dramatic details of the plight of the lost son and of the joyful partying on his return, the major movement/content of the stories are the same. The continued searching is suggested by the fact that the father is already waiting, sees the son, and runs to meet him, and especially that the father's action does not wait upon but anticipates the son's carefully rehearsed speech (of repentance? 18-19). When the son finally is able to get to his speech (21), the father's party instructions interrupt him before he can get to the part about becoming a hired servant. He is still a son! "This is my son," the father says, who was "dead" and who has now come to life again, who was lost and is now found (24). Thus to the theme of lost and found, is added that of death and coming alive, in apparent anticipation of the themes of death and resurrection that will culminate this journey and this story, with the same response of "joy" that greets the son who is now alive, belonging then to the gathered disciples in Jerusalem (24:41).

Finally, the repetition of "dead" and "alive" in vv. 24 and 32 accents the theme, while the second occurrence adds to it the note of necessity. "It was necessary" (NRSV "we had to") to rejoice. In Luke's vocabulary and within his story, this joy in the recovery of the lost is as necessary as it is that the Christ should suffer and die and rise again (cf. 24:7, 26, 46). As such it is a clue to the purposes of God.

Thus it is significant that this third part of the story introduces the important feature that the one not lost has a speaking part. How do those who are not lost, who do not need repentance, respond to the continuous seeking and searching and joy? Do those who "need no repentance" become angry as if excluded? Do they refuse to join as friends and neighbors in the extension of the joy? Do they instead take their place alongside the Pharisees and scribes who find that it is precisely this invitation to joy at the recovery of even one sinner that is just what they don't like about this Jesus?

Eighteenth Sunday after Pentecost
Twenty-Fifth Sunday in Ordinary Time/Proper 20

Lectionary	First Lesson	Psalm	Second Lesson	Gospel
Revised Common	Amos 8:4-7 or Jer. 8:18—9:1	Psalm 113 or 79:1-9	I Tim. 2:1-7	Luke 16:1-13
Episcopal (BCP)	Amos 8:4-7, (8-12)	Psalm 138	I Tim. 2:1-8	Luke 16:1-13
Roman Catholic	Amos 8:4-7	Ps. 113:1-2, 4-8	I Tim. 2:1-8	Luke 16:1-13 or 16:10-13
Lutheran (LBW)	Amos 8:4-7	Psalm 113	I Tim. 2:1-8	Luke 16:1-13

FIRST LESSON: AMOS 8:4-7, (8-12); JEREMIAH 8:18—9:1

Amos 8:4-7, (8-12). In a time of economic prosperity and security during the long reign of Jereboam II (786–746 B.C.E.) the prophet Amos was called by God to cross over from Judah to Israel in the north to speak a word of judgment upon the excesses of the people.

After symmetrical pronouncements against Israel, Judah, and their neighbors (chaps. 1–2; "For three transgressions . . . and for four . . .") and three oracles on Israel's sins and God's punishment (chaps. 3–6; "Hear this word . . ."), Amos describes a series of visions that God showed him of God's judgment on Israel and the coming destruction (7:1—9:15; locusts, fire, a plumb line, a basket of fruit, and the Lord standing by the altar). The fourth of these visions, a basket of summer fruit, is the reading for this Sunday.

The point of the vision depends on a wordplay on the Hebrew word for fruit, *qayits*, and the similarly sounding *qets*, which means "end." As the Lord's interpretation makes clear (2-3), the vision has to do not with the "end time" of harvest, but with an end time of destruction in which songs of joy will be turned into dirges at the piling up of dead bodies (3).

The oracle of the Lord that follows (4-14) elaborates on the reason—the destruction of the poor and needy of the land by greedy and deceitful tactics of buying and selling. The cruelty of the rich is no matter of chance oversight; they can't wait for the Sabbath to end to get back to their shady practices. Ironically, they have gone so far from God they cannot even be comfortably hypocritical and deceitfully religious.

Such irony does not escape God. As terrible as their deeds, so shall their judgment be. "I will never forget any of their deeds" (7). Though perhaps a dreadful-sounding place to end the reading, there is no softening in the extension of the reading through v. 12, where reference is made to the day of the Lord (9). Far from a time of hoped-for blessing, that day will be a time of utter destruction, when feasting will be turned into mourning and lamentation into a famine not of bread or water, but of "hearing the words of the Lord."

Like Amos' prophecy as a whole, this reading calls for concern for the poor and needy so easily trampled upon, especially in times of economic prosperity when satisfaction of wants seems to breed not concern for the other but the creation of more wants. Second, by negative example it calls for a connection between the religious observance of the presence of God and responsibility for the poor and needy in our midst. The people of Amos's time had severed that connection in their scrambling after gain. The announcement, yes, the promise of God, is that God will not forget or leave unpunished such evil deeds. The ultimate threat is that the withdrawal of God's presence will lead to a desert of body and spirit tantamount to death.

Jeremiah 8:18—9:1. Whereas Amos warns of a famine of the Lord's presence, Jeremiah at a later time laments having pronounced a judgment that is already taking place. Captive Israel is no longer, and now the destruction of Jerusalem is imminent.

Sick with grief and with tears that fail to match the number of the people slain in the destruction, four times Jeremiah's refrain of "my poor people" is joined to a different aspect of the destruction's sorrow and suffering: the "cry" (19); the "hurt" (21; crushing); the "healing" that will not come (22); and the heaps of the "slain" (9:1).

The same double sense of "end" that occasioned Amos's vision occurs here. The summer (*qayits*) is over, but the end has brought not a harvest of health and fruit, but only more sickness and destruction. Explicit in Jeremiah's lament are deep questions about the actions of God. The "famine" Amos anticipates is now the reality of Jeremiah's experience. Can it be that the Lord is not really in Zion? That Jerusalem's king is gone? Is there really no healing balm in Gilead to end the suffering of Jeremiah's people?

When the people suffer, Jeremiah feels their pain and their anguish. As the reading continues, his anguish deepens when he is compelled to speak the word of the Lord's judgment as not capricious but consistent with the evil and deceitful ways of the people. God's punishment is just, but it is not for that reason any easier to bear. Both Jeremiah and we still long for some healing that will alleviate the suffering and the sense of abandonment by God.

SECOND LESSON: I TIMOTHY 2:1-8

As in last Sunday's reading, a creedal formulation is the basis for the exhortation that initiates chap. two; it is worthy of the preacher's focus.

The litmus test for all teaching is the confession that God is savior, who wills that all people be saved and come to the knowledge of the truth (3-4). Salvation and true knowledge are further specified and secured from idle speculation in the confession that God is one, and that there is only one mediator of salvation between God and humankind, namely Jesus Christ, who was also human and gave himself as a ransom on behalf of all people (5-6a).

Two further assertions surround this central confession. The first in order of logic is Paul's following assertion that for the purpose of "witness" (NRSV "attestation") "at the right time" he was appointed preacher ("herald," *keryx*), apostle, and teacher of the Gentiles in matters of "faith" and "truth" (6b-7). These short verses argue for the emerging close tie between confession and apostleship, between true doctrine and commissioned leaders, that will come to mark the Christian church more strongly in the next centuries. They raise the question, How best may that "knowledge of truth" that is not just idle speculation or false doctrine, but constitutive of the appropriation of God's will for salvation for all people, be secured and brought to fruition in each contemporary context?

Second, if Paul is appointed apostle, preacher, and teacher of "faith and truth," then his opening concern is also central: the exercise of the discipline of prayer within the community (1-2). Prayer as discipline is suggested by the urging of its constancy and by the careful distinctions of its different types: specific petitions (NRSV "supplications"), prayers, intercessions, and thanksgivings. It is further instructive that this community is encouraged to prayer on behalf of "all people," including (significantly because especially named) kings and *all* those who are in positions of leadership or authority. The goal of such prayer is that people will be enabled to the "leading" of a "peaceable and quiet life" in godliness and dignity (2), a goal directly linked to the will of God for salvation asserted in the creedal formula that follows.

The overarching concern of the instructions throughout this chapter is for the preservation of life in good order and "quietness" (*hesychia*, one of the common philosophic virtues, 2, 11). That concern extends then to specific instructions about the roles of men and women, as the "then" and the balancing of "men" in v. 8 with "women" in v. 9 makes clear. The problematic character of the ensuing instructions about the silence of women in the community, about the character of dress that is properly reverent, and the exhortations to silence and prohibitions of women having authority over men certainly occasions the lectionary decision to stop at v. 8 and thus to distort the clear structural ties between v. 8 and vv. 9f. This discomfort also stems from the strange exegetical application of the Genesis account through talk about the "order" of Adam and Eve's creation, the "deception of Eve," and "salvation through childbirth" provided that women continue in "faith," "love," "holiness," and "modesty," that is, in possession of all the central moral virtues (15). This last list simply underscores what has been said above about the central concern of this text for peace and quiet and moral order that should characterize this community as it lives in the world.

One must, of course, reject the particular exegesis as misdirected, and the prohibitions regarding the mutual roles of men and women as culturally and contextually determined. At the same time one recognizes the validity of the confession of centrality of God's salvation in Jesus Christ, and the urging to prayer that this salvation should be effective for all people in lives lived daily in reverence and in good order and peace.

GOSPEL: LUKE 16:1-13

As Jesus' teaching in parables continues (see the Seventeenth Sunday after Pentecost), he now turns abruptly to address directly the "disciples" on the journey. The reading may be divided into several parts: (*a*) the parable proper concluding with the master's commendation of the "steward of unrighteousness" (1-8; NRSV, "dishonest steward"); (*b*) Jesus' teaching application of the parable (9); followed by (*c*) a series of sayings on faithfulness and serving (10-13). Verses 14-15, describing the response of the Pharisees to Jesus' teaching, are linked thematically to the reading by talk of "righteousness."

The details of the parable are clear for the most part, but certain matters deserve caution. The traditional title of "dishonest steward" appears nowhere in the text. In fact, what we hear instead is the master's commendation of the steward for acting "prudently" or "shrewdly." At least he should be called the "shrewd steward." To do so alters our hearing, particularly of the opening scene. When we are told that "charges were brought" to the rich owner that his steward was squandering his property, the parable in no way assumes that these charges are true. The word translated "charges were brought" normally means "falsely or slanderously." Thus, if any assumptions are to be made, it is that the charges are trumped up. The actions of the steward are those of one who has been drummed out of his position by false accusations, and who now has to plan quickly to secure the future because of an unjust turn of events. This does not "excuse" his actions, but certainly puts a different perspective on their evaluation by the hearer.

It is not clear whether the rewriting of the bills means that the steward retains the difference or that he now is owed favors from those debtors whose bills have been reduced. In any case, the assumption is clear that he has secured his own future. This is underscored by the fact that the rich man (suddenly called "master," *kyrios*, probably in a subtle transition to Jesus' teaching to follow) now commends this steward for having "acted shrewdly" (8). In his actions he is further described as a "steward of unrighteouness" (not "dishonest manager"; for similar uses of the phrase cf. "stewards of God's mysteries," 1 Cor. 4:1; "stewards of God's grace," 1 Pet. 4:10; and so forth). That is to say, he is one who "manages matters of unrighteousness" prudently. The word order in Luke's narrative is instructive: the master literally commended him "as steward of *unrighteousness* because *prudently* he acted." It is significant that unrighteousness and prudence are thus juxtaposed, while the "steward's actions" provide an enclosing framework for the associated alternatives. We hearers are meant to contemplate the apparent juxtaposition of opposites, to think the unthinkable, and that is part of the jarring character of this parable.

In Jesus' application or teaching (8-9), this jarring character is not relieved. Far from exhorting us to beware of the ways of the world, we "disciples"—that is, the "children of light" (cf. John 12:36; Eph. 5:8; 1 Thess. 5:5; though naturally suggesting contrast with "children of darkness," here used in contrast to "children of this age," implying as well that "children of light" are ones who belong not to this age but to the future)— are encouraged to have at least as much wisdom in handling the matters (wealth) of this world (of unrighteousness) in order that, when it fails, we will have a place in the "eternal" dwelling places.

Jesus' teaching now includes a series of proverbial sayings depending on contrasts of little and much, unjust and true, the other's and one's own, and serving two masters (10-13). The series is linked by themes recurring from the parable: "faithfulness" (*pistos*); "entrusting" (*pisteuo*); or "truth" is juxtaposed to "unfaithfulness" or "dishonesty" (*adikos, adikia*). The final saying brings us back full circle to the beginning of the reading. Though a different word, *mammon*, is used, it is thematically tied to the issue of "wealth" at the opening: a certain man was "rich."

This connection is confirmed and clarified when the Pharisees are said to overhear these words of Jesus and to make fun of him "because they were *lovers of money*" (14-15). These themes have been brought together around the issue of money (see Luke 16:19-31 and notes on the Nineteenth Sunday after Pentecost). Second, Jesus refers to them as ones who "justify" themselves before others in this world, but whose hearts appear much different to God who "knows the heart."

This puzzling parable encourages us through apparent reversals to think about appearances and what constitutes righteousness and faithfulness in contrast to injustice in this world. Our standards of what is right and wrong, our understanding of what discipleship calls for in this world, are often confused and without the wisdom that should belong to "children of the light." The perspective of God's good news in Jesus means that we look at this world through a different lens. Prudent actions of disciples whose future belongs not to this age but to the "eternal" age should be at least as wise as those who make use of the resources of this world for the future. Above all, faithfulness that counts is that which is characterized by service, first of all to God, and then of course to one another.

Nineteenth Sunday after Pentecost

Twenty-Sixth Sunday in Ordinary Time/Proper 21

Lectionary	First Lesson	Psalm	Second Lesson	Gospel
Revised Common	Amos 6:1a, 4-7 or Jer. 32:1-3a, 6-15	Psalm 146 or Ps. 91:1-6, 14-16	I Tim. 6:6-19	Luke 16:19-31
Episcopal (BCP)	Amos 6:1-7	Psalm 146 or Ps. 146:4-9	I Tim. 6:11-19	Luke 16:19-31
Roman Catholic	Amos 6:1a, 4-7	Ps. 146:2, 7-10	I Tim. 6:11-16	Luke 16:19-31
Lutheran (LBW)	Amos 6:1-7	Psalm 146	I Tim. 6:6-16	Luke 16:19-31

FIRST LESSON: AMOS 6:1-7; JEREMIAH 32:1-3a, 6-15

Amos 6:1-7. Today's lesson will be difficult for the preacher who looks in vain for some hidden word of good news or hope tucked amid the message of unrelenting judgment. The beginning, with its mournful "woe" of a funeral dirge, anticipates the cries of suffering and anguish that will be exchanged at the end for the joyful and false revelry of the "loungers." The structure of the lesson is of an ever-increasing specificity corresponding to the heightening sense of outrage at the luxurious living of the leaders. Their present false sense of "security" and "ease" plays against the background of the coming and sure destruction, a sign not only of their blindness but of their outright disregard for the implications of their actions.

Though v. 1's third-person discourse allows the hearers to remain as it were in ease and security, v. 2 addresses the hearers directly, challenging their complacency and their blindness. If the "first ones" are blind, then the examples are plain enough to see. "Just go and look! Open your eyes!" the negative examples say, concluding with the "land of *you*" that brings the message home (see the NIV's correct translation of the Hebrew text; the NRSV adopts an emended reading).

The address now becomes specific in a series of parallel addresses (3-6), each beginning identically with a participle whose direct address is shaped by the "you" that ends v. 2. The effective beginning of each verse is thus: "you ones who . . ." (this fact the NRSV disguises by its unfounded addition of "alas" in v. 4, thus implying a new section, and by its use of the third-person "those who" for the address of vv. 4-6).

Several levels of irony are couched in the balanced phrasing of v. 3: that in the "putting far away" out of mind and reality, they are actually "bringing near" violence and destruction, and that in imagining they can put off the "end" of that "evil day" they in fact propel the arrival of God's swift judgment upon their cruel and indifferent behavior. Thus the violence they bring on is twofold: (1) the violence is worked on the poor and the power-less by their indifference and luxurious behaviors; and (2) the violence will come upon them, and tragically on the poor and powerless as well, in the coming destruction of defeat and exile.

This double sense of violence makes all the more atrocious the callous actions of the leaders. While they wine and dine luxuriously on ivory couches, drunkenly fumbling at the harp strings and doing cheap imitations of David, anointing themselves with the "finest oils" (literally "first," that is, the same word as used in vv. 1 and 7, and thus a reminder of the ironic play on this word that runs through the lesson), it bothers them not one whit that the cheap imitations of their "idle" songs have perverted the deep piety and worship of God as shown in the psalms of David, and further that their actions will become the occasion of the destruction of Joseph—the nation (4-6).

This reference to the ruin of Joseph in the last line of v. 6 leads directly to the final word of judgment marked by an emphatic initial "Therefore now" (split by the NRSV). Return to the third-person "they" accents the harshness and the "distancing" from God implied in the double refrain of "going into exile" and "passing away." Meanwhile, since in their ease they have found security in their desire to be "first," even now in their judgment their desires will be ironically granted in that they will be granted the "honor" of going "first" into exile. The judgment anticipated in v. 1 has now come full circle. We are to imagine that the mournful cry of "woe" of the captives has supplanted the songs of revelry, just as the plodding, wea-ried feet and parched lips have supplanted the lounging and rich feasts.

Jeremiah 32:1-3a, 6-15. Jeremiah's prophecy, coming over a century-and-a-half later than that of Amos, when Judah is poised before its imminent capture and exile, is similarly persistent in its message of the Lord's pun-ishment for the disobedience of the nation and particularly its leaders. Yet Jeremiah holds out some measure of hope that the people will repent and that, having served out their sentence of exile, there will come a restora-tion, a new covenant marked by a people with an obedient and faithful heart. Then they will experience the depth of God's forgiving love and the tangible evidence of God's favor in the rebuilding of the city (31:23-40).

Today's lesson picks up with Nebuchadrezzar besieging Jerusalem (see Jeremiah 37 for the narrative background). Political intrigue is betting on one counselor or another and weighing the chances of defeat. The lesson skips over Jeremiah's warning to King Zedekiah that there is nothing he can do to escape the Lord's judgment (3b-5) and focuses on Jeremiah's purchase of a piece of family property. The meticulous details of the trans-action while the defeat and exile of the nation are so close at hand bear witness to the faithfulness of the Lord's promise of the return and restoration of Judah and Jerusalem. As sure as this promise is, it is also clear that it will not happen immediately; the instructions are to make preparations for the deeds "so that they will last a long time." In case the object lesson fails to make the point, Jeremiah through his aide Baruch adds the final rationale ("For," 15) that the actions anticipate the certain fulfillment of the word of the Lord. Life will return to its former shape. Houses and fields and vineyards will again be bought and sold in the land.

Jeremiah calls for trusting the steadfast love of God just when things seem most bleak and hope most distant. Coming just as the enemy is perched at the gates of Jerusalem, his words put that trust to their most severe test. Not many were able to hear and believe Jeremiah's message at the time. The question for us is, Do we need to experience the same disaster as the people of Judah before we can believe that such restoration or deliverance is real?

SECOND LESSON: I TIMOTHY 6:6-19

Today's reading belongs to the conclusion of the letter and to a thematically and structurally linked unit divided as follows:

1. Teach and urge these things . . . (2-10)
2. Flee these things, but pursue . . . (11-16)
3. Command them . . . (17-19)
4. Guard what has been entrusted . . . (20-21)

The first three of these sections have the sequence of "what you are to teach," "what the manner of your own life should be," and "what you should command to others." Their common theme is riches or wealth (*ploutos* in various forms occurs more than five times) in contrast to "godliness" (*eusebeia*, 2, 5, 6, 11).

"Godliness" means to live in "accordance with the sound [healthy] words of the Lord Jesus Christ" (3). Apparently some depraved members of the community find "godliness" to be profitable (a "means of gain," 4-5), but true godliness is recognized by its "contentment" (*autarkia*, the word is beloved by Cynics and Stoics, 6). Wanting wealth, then, is the snare that leads to ruin, as the familiar quotation now summarizes it: "the love of money is root of all evils" (10).

Section 2 warns Timothy to flee from such "evils" and to pursue righteousness, now linked through the word *godliness* to faith, love, endurance, and so forth (11). To be faithful is to "fight the good fight" (*agon* is metaphorical language of an athletic contest), the prize at the end of which is eternal life, the result of one's "calling" and making of a "good confession" (12) in the presence of many witnesses. That good confession is modeled on the example of Jesus Christ, who indeed made the "good confession" (13) before Pontius Pilate. With mention of Jesus' confession, the exhortation turns to confession of Jesus Christ as Lord, concluding in the formulaic "Amen" of doxology. This second section thus begins with the command to pursue godliness and ends with the doxological ascription of supreme godliness to the example and exaltation of Jesus Christ as Lord. Again, the teaching and example of the "Lord Jesus Christ" (cf. 3, 14f.) is the guarantee of sound teaching as well as of a righteous life for those who would be leaders in the community of faith.

Verses 17-19 return from the perspective of the heavenly heights and the "eternal dominion" (16) to this "present age" and the theme that occupied the first section: wealth. In fact the word *wealth* verbally takes over, with no less than four occurrences in these three verses. In contrast to the "godliness with contentment" held up in the first section, we hear now of wealth too readily joined to a haughtiness that places its hopes on the uncertainty of wealth (6). Hope, rather, is founded on the recognition that wealth is a gift from God "who richly provides all things for our enjoyment." Thus this lesson calls not for the avoidance or despising of wealth, but rather the avoidance of that longing for or desiring of wealth (8) or that "love of money" that is the root of evil (10). On the contrary, the "wealthy" are called to use wealth in doing good works, showing their true riches in those good deeds that are exhibited in examples of "sharing" and "partnership in community" (*eumetadous, koinonikous,* 18). By so doing they are "storing up" for themselves a treasure" (19) for the future, that will be marked by their taking hold of "life that is really life."

The reference to such a "treasure" (NRSV, "what has been entrusted") links section 4 (20-21) to the "treasure" of v. 19. This treasure is what Timothy is finally instructed to guard; the letter's conclusion thus combines this more immediate instruction about true riches with the concern for sound teaching and true knowledge that is the "mark of faith."

GOSPEL: LUKE 16:19-31

The common theme of wealth or riches links the Gospel for today to the parable of last Sunday's lesson (see the remarks on 16:14-15 in the Eighteenth Sunday after Pentecost) as well as to the readings from Amos and 1 Timothy. That which counts for many as a matter of loftiness or boasting (the same root word as in 1 Tim. 6:17, "haughty") is contrasted to what God knows about what is "stored up as treasure" in the heart. Jesus' sayings on the law and the prophets (16-17) and on divorce and adultery (18) anticipate the conclusion of today's parable with its question about the sufficiency of hearing "Moses and the prophets" (29, 31) for the obedience and persuasion of faith (NRSV "be convinced," *peitho*). The "time" of the law and the prophets is clearly contrasted with that of the proclamation of the good news of the kingdom of God (16). Already suggested in the steward who craftily makes careful plans for his future (1-13), now in this subsequent parable the issue of the interrelation of affairs and actions in and with the stuff of this world with the status or character of the afterlife becomes pressed more earnestly.

The parable is a troubling one; its four scenes starkly contrast the "fortunes" of its two main characters, a contrast made more extreme in that only the "rich man" in the parable remains nameless throughout.

Scene 1 (19-21) sets the background for the surprising reversals that will come in the next scene. The translations mask the explicit contrast of character ("A certain man was rich"; "a certain [man was] poor") and situation ("*dressed* in finery"; literally "*thrown* [*ballo*] at his gate"). The "dressing" and constant "feasting" of the rich man is explicit in the phrase "every day" and in the Greek imperfect/present tenses of ongoing or persistent good fortune, while the Greek perfect underscores the complete and final hopelessness of the poor man's being "thrown at the gate" and "covered with sores." We hear the pathetic hopelessness of his "continuous longing" (again present tense) just even once to "be satisfied" (Greek aorist of specific event), not with the luxurious food of the feasting that lies across the divide (the "but" literally divides vv. 19 and 20 and the two characters from one another) but with the "things" that (again "constantly") fall from the rich man's table. The student of Scripture will recall the Canaanite woman of Matt. 15:27. Whereas there dogs eat the *crumbs* that fall from the master's table, here the poor man "eats" the *things* (not even crumbs of food) that fall from the rich man's table, while the dogs instead persistently lick (again Greek imperfect) the poor man's sores!

Scene 2 (22-23) details the reversal of fates both in content and order: Scene 1's order of rich man → poor man becomes now poor man → rich man ("the last first and the first last"? cf. Luke 13:30), though both "die" ("also") and so are alike in their mortality. The poor man, however, is "carried" by angels into Abraham's bosom; the rich man is "buried," period! The torments of Hades become the occasion for the rich man now for the first time actually to "look up" and "see" Lazarus, now in Abraham's bosom. His fate has taught him to see in a way that his previous wealth and feasting had prevented.

In scene 3 (24-26) this comforting (at least for the moralist in us) reversal has a discomforting sequel. The liturgically and religiously appropriate plea, "Have mercy on me," meets outright rejection (cf. *kyrie eleison*). In spite of the rich man's prayer for just one cool touch of water on his tongue (the verbs are all aorist of specific event) to break the constant agony (present linear) of "this flame" (not "flames" as in the NRSV; the pain focuses the experience in its singularity!), Abraham denies the request. In painful irony, while addressing the man for the first time in the story as anything but "rich" (he is now at last but too late a "child"), Abraham pronounces a blessing on the reversal of fortune. The reversal is confirmed by the orders of creation: a great chasm (*chasma mega*) "has been fixed" (the perfect tense underscores its permanence). At this point of finality all hope should be gone, and the narrative should end. But it does not.

Instead, scene 4 begins with a "therefore" of resignation and change of tactics. The rich man in torment turns from a plea for mercy for himself to intercession on behalf of the members of his family (*adelphoi*). He asks for one sent to "bear a thorough *witness*" (NRSV "warn," *diamartyreo,* is questionable for Luke; cf. Acts 2:40; 8:25; 10:42; 18:5; 20:21, 23, 24; 28:23, where it is consistently not "warning" but the proclamation and witness to the good news of the gospel of Jesus Christ) so that they may not come to the same end of "torment" (note the link to scene 3 in v. 23).

Surprisingly (are we not a bit troubled?), Abraham's response to this intercession is again a flat rejection. The issue clearly turns to that of "hearing," and the response of faith and obedience, and on what basis that will take place. Let them hear Moses and the prophets, Abrahams replies, and his rejection is not overturned by repeated pleas.

In the accompanying reference to one rising from the dead and to the subsequent repentance such a resurrection would occasion we anticipate where this story is leading us. Indeed, at the end of this journey of discipleship (the "goes" of v. 30 is a verbal reminder of this journey), the speaker of this parable will die and be raised from the dead. Then the question will be put to those who hear, whether on the basis of Moses and the prophets it will be enough for faith to be born (cf. the Emmaus disciples in 24:27).

Certainly this parable is troubling. The issue is not resolved here, nor is it resolved at the end of the Gospel. There, in the narrative of the resurrection, finally it is Jesus himself who must "open the minds" of the disciples (24:44) and who alone by the promise of the gift of the Holy Spirit can occasion the witness of this community to the repentance and forgiveness that come in the name of this resurrected one.

In the meantime, this parable, in its talk of wealth (just as Amos sees judgment as a confirmation of the hardness of heart and the ignorance of those who lounge and feast), only makes permanent a divide that has already been expressed in actions of complete disregard by the wealthy here and now. These lessons invite the question of what it will take for such hard-heartedness to be healed. They direct us to the hope that resides in the witness to one who comes to rise from the dead and lead a community of those who have been convinced and changed, whose lives have experienced a different kind of reversal than that which this parable describes. As 1 Timothy suggests, such a community is called not to abandon their wealth, but to be "good at distribution" (*eumetadotos*) in the partnership of sharing (*koinonous*) in the gospel. Such sharing can only come from those who recognize and have experienced that treasure that finds it foundation in the promise of life that belongs not to the things of this world but to the consolation that is ours in Jesus Christ.